for men only

a straightforward guide
to the inner lives of women

by Shaunti and Jeff Feldhahn

Multnomah® Publishers *Sisters, Oregon*

FOR MEN ONLY
published by Multnomah Publishers, Inc.
Published in association with Calvin W. Edwards,
Post Office Box 88472, Atlanta, GA 30356
© 2006 by Veritas Enterprises, Inc.

International Standard Book Number: 1-59052-572-8

Cover design by Studiogearbox.com
Cover photo by PixelWorks Studios, www.shootpw.com
Interior design and typeset by Katherine Lloyd, The DESK

Unless otherwise indicated, Scripture quotations are from:
The Holy Bible, New International Version
© 1973, 1984 by International Bible Society,
used by permission of Zondervan Publishing House

Multnomah is a trademark of Multnomah Publishers, Inc.,
and is registered in the U.S. Patent and Trademark Office.
The colophon is a trademark of Multnomah Publishers, Inc.
Printed in the United States of America

MULTNOMAH PUBLISHERS, INC.
601 N. LARCH STREET • SISTERS, OREGON 97759

Library of Congress Cataloging-in-Publication Data
Feldhahn, Shaunti Christine.
For men only / by Shaunti and Jeff Feldhahn.
     p. cm.
  ISBN 1-59052-572-8
  1. Men (Christian theology) 2. Christian men--Conduct of life.
I. Feldhahn, Jeff. II. Title.
  BT703.5.F45 2006
  248.8'42--dc22
                                                                    2006000677
             06 07 08 09 10—10 9 8 7 6 5 4 3 2 1 0

To our parents;
Who taught us through their example
that working to understand one another
is worth it

Contents

A note from Shaunti, to women readers:

I want to give a warm greeting—and an important caution—to any curious fellow females peeking in at what we're telling guys about how we are wired!

As Jeff and I have talked to couples about the subjects of both this book and my previous book, *For Women Only*, we've seen a need for caution in how men and women handle each other's expectations afterward. Because men and women are processing these new findings about each other very, very differently.

Women tend to process things by talking them through. So when women read or listen to the findings in *For Women Only*, they often turn to their husband or boyfriend and say (usually in astonishment), "Is this *true?*" Which leads to a lively conversation, and a feeling of new closeness with their man.

Men, however, tend to process things by thinking them through, and not saying *anything* until they fully understand what they are thinking. So, when men read or listen to the findings in *For Men Only*, they usually get real quiet. They are processing internally, and simply aren't capable of talking about it for some time—or maybe much at all. Which…*doesn't* lead to a lively conversation!

This key difference could lead to disappointment if

women didn't know to expect it. We could easily think, "He didn't learn anything about me," or even, "He must not care about me."

In our experience, neither is true. It is so hard to do, but if we women will let men have the time to process, we've found that while men may or may not *talk* about what they learned, they usually start *doing* it.

So in the days and weeks after your loved one reads any part of this book, keep your eyes open to recognize and affirm when that happens!

—*Shaunti*

Chapter 1

RETHINKING RANDOM

Why you need a new map of the female universe

ike some guys I know, you might be tempted to skip this introduction and jump right to the sex chapter. And if you're chuckling right now, it probably means you already did it. Or were about to.

It's not a bad choice, actually. Just a little self-defeating. If you've been in a committed relationship with a woman for more than, say, a day, you know that going just for what you want isn't actually going to get you what you want for very long.

A week, maybe?

But let's be honest—one of the main reasons you're looking at this book is that you *are* trying to get something you want. Not sex (well, not *just* sex), but a more fulfilling, harmonious relationship with your wife, one that isn't quite so hard or confusing. And the back cover gave you the wild idea that understanding her *might* actually be possible.

Either that, or for some reason, the woman in question just handed you this book.

Hmmm.

Well, either way, take a look at the revelations we've uncovered. We think you'll be convinced. Each chapter explains things about the woman you love that may have often left you feeling helpless, confused, or just plain angry. Each chapter points out simple, doable solutions. The only genius required is that you make a decision up front that you're willing to think differently. This is a short book, but if you read it cover to cover, you'll walk away with your eyes opened to things you may have never before understood about your wife or girlfriend.

Each chapter points out simple, doable solutions.

That's what happened with me—Jeff. And I'm just your average, semi-confused guy. (Actually, sometimes totally confused is more accurate.) And since us average, semi-confused guys have to stick together, that's why, even though Shaunti and I are both authoring this book, I'll be the one doing most of the talking.

First, Some Background

In 2004 Shaunti published *For Women Only: What You Need to Know About the Inner Lives of Men*, which quickly became a bestseller. Based on a nationally representative survey, scores of focus groups, and other research, it opened women's eyes to things that most of us guys had always wished our wives knew. Things like, most of us need to feel *respected* even more than loved. Or besides just getting enough sex, men also have a huge need to feel sexually *desired* by our wives.

I'm not sure exactly why, but women everywhere were shocked. To me, those revelations seemed obvious. But by the flood of letters from around the country—from both women *and* their grateful husbands—we've seen how much good can come when the opposite sex finally has their eyes opened to things they simply didn't understand before.

> I'm not sure exactly why, but women everywhere were shocked by how men thought.

In this book, the shock is on the other foot. Now it's been Shaunti's turn to say, over and over, "I can't believe you didn't already know that!"

When Shaunti's publisher first approached us about doing a companion to *For Women Only* to help men understand women, I had two major concerns. First, I didn't think guys would read a "relationship" book since, for most of us, the last relationship book we read was in premarital counseling—and then only because we were forced to. But more to the point, I doubted that a woman could ever be understood. Compared to other complex matters—like the tides, say, or how to figure a baseball player's ERA—women seemed unknowable. Random even.

I explained my skepticism to one early focus group of women:

Jeff: Guys tend to think that women are random. We think, *I pulled this lever last week and got a certain reaction. But when I pulled that same lever this week, I got a totally different reaction.* That's random!

Woman in group: But we aren't random! If you pull the lever and get a different reaction, either you're pulling a different lever, or you're pulling it in a different way.

Shaunti: What men need is a sort of map to their wives. Because we can be mapped. We can be known and understood terrain.

Jeff: See, guys think of a woman as a swamp: You can't see where you're stepping, and sooner or later you just know you're going to get stuck in quicksand. And the more you struggle to get free, the deeper you get sucked in. So every guy on the planet knows that the best thing to do is just shut down and hope somebody comes along to rescue you.

When I came to, Shaunti and the other women in the focus group assured me—and I have since seen for myself—that guys don't have to live in a swamp. That realization led us to the eventual subtitle of this book: "A Straightforward Guide to the Inner Lives of Women."

> "Guys think of a woman as a swamp: You can't see where you're stepping, and sooner or later you just know you're going to get stuck in quicksand."

The Seven Revelations

The most important key to "de-swamping" the woman in your life is to realize that some of your basic assumptions about her may be either too simplistic or flat wrong. By simplistic, I mean that we tend to operate with a partial or surface understanding of our wife or girlfriend. And to make matters worse, most guys have no idea how to make their limited understanding work in actual practice.

For example, most guys have heard that women want security. Okay—but what does that mean, exactly? A regular paycheck? A big house? A growing retirement fund? It's a huge shocker to talk to hundreds of women and find that while financial security is nice, it isn't nearly as important to them as feeling emotionally secure—feeling close and confident that you will be there for her no matter what. And believe it or not, ensuring emotional security turns out to be a lot easier than ensuring the financial security you are probably busting your tail to provide.

For Men Only will help you move from surface understandings to the all-important recognition of what those things mean in everyday life with your woman. Once you start testing out these findings, I think you'll be amazed at the difference it makes for both of you.

> *For Men Only* will help you move from surface understanding to recognizing what those things mean in everyday life.

The book is organized around six major findings outlined on the next page. Some of these will be surprises to you. Some won't, at least to begin with. (But that's the thing about "swamps"—what you see is rarely what is really there.)

OUR SURFACE UNDERSTANDING	*WHAT IT MEANS IN PRACTICE*
Women need to feel loved.	Even if your relationship is great, your mate likely has a fundamental insecurity about your love—and when that insecurity is triggered, she may respond in ways that confuse or dismay you until she feels reassured.
Women are emotional.	Women deal with multiple thoughts and emotions from their past and present all the time, at the same time—and these can't be easily dismissed.
Women want security— in other words, financial security.	Your woman needs emotional security and closeness with you so much that she will endure financial insecurity to get it.
She doesn't want you to fix it; she just wants you to listen.	When she is sharing an emotional problem, her feelings and her desire to be heard are much more important than the problem itself.
She doesn't want much sex; she must not want me.	Physically, women tend to crave sex less often than men do—and it is usually not related to your desirability.
She wants to look attractive.	Inside your smart, secure wife lives a little girl who deeply needs to know that you find her beautiful—and that you only have eyes for her.

Intro

How We Found Out: Our Methodology

For nearly a year, Shaunti and I worked to identify inner "map terrain" areas that are common to most women but that most guys tend not to understand. Besides conducting hundreds of in-person interviews, we gathered huge amounts of anecdotal information at dozens of women's events where Shaunti was presenting materials from *For Women Only*. I spoke with stay-at-home moms, business owners, and secretaries; on airplanes, in focus groups, and over Shaunti's book table as she was mobbed after women's conferences. And I sifted through hundreds of e-mails and forum postings from Shaunti's 4-womenonly.com website.

In all these venues, I was really just the "embedded male." Like the reporters who rode with the armored cavalry divisions at the opening of the Iraqi war, I kept my helmet on, my head down, and my notebook handy.

> I was the "embedded male." I kept my helmet on, my head down, and my notebook handy.

After all that research, we did a scientific national survey. As Shaunti had done for her previous book, we worked with survey-design expert Chuck Cowan, former chief of census design for the U.S. Census Bureau, and professional survey company Decision Analyst. They came together to help us design and conduct a groundbreaking, representative survey of four hundred women all over the country. In the end, between interviews, surveys, events, and other input, we estimate that well over three thousand women provided input for this book.

I know you'll be fascinated by the results. While some of the findings may be challenging or difficult to accept, most men have been surprised by how helpful many of these truths are and how *simple* they are to implement for a better, easier relationship.

The Map Key

Before we tackle each of the findings, some pointers on read-ing the map:

- **This book holds to a biblical world view.** Our aim is to be relevant and revealing, no matter what your worldview is. But because Shaunti and I view life through our Christian faith, we have seen that these findings are consistent with bibli-cal principles. We believe that relationships are most fulfilling when both people have a common commitment to serving Jesus Christ. We do not quote very heavily from Scripture, but we do draw from and reference it as the only truly dependable guidebook for relationships. For example, our starting-point assumption is that husbands need to love their wives just as Jesus does us—which means to love, serve, and be willing to sacrifice everything for her good, even above our own.

- **This is not a comprehensive marriage book.** There are already plenty of marriage books on the market—including many terrific ones from Christian experts. So we stay away from well-covered topics and areas that guys already tend to have a handle on, and we leave the heavy-duty theological discussions for those books. (If you want to investigate those further, we list several recommended resources at our website, www.formenonlybook.com.) Also, while we are writing more for married men, these insights will be helpful for anyone in a committed male-female relationship. That said, if your relationship is seriously on the rocks, this little book will probably open your eyes in some important areas, but it is not designed to cover a real crisis situation. We encourage you to get the kind of counsel and support your marriage deserves.

- **This is not an equal treatment.** Just as *For Women Only* was purposefully one-sided—and if your wife read it, you may have benefited from that fact—so is this book. Yes, you have needs too, and there certainly may be relationship issues arising because *she* doesn't understand *you*. But *For Women Only* addresses many of those, and this book is not about them. This is only about the inner lives of women, and we're focusing entirely on how men relate to women, not the other way around. (That is also why the survey only polled heterosexual women.)

- **There are exceptions to every rule.** Recognize that when I say "most women" appear to think a certain way, "most" does not mean all. We make generalizations out of necessity to be helpful in the widest number of circumstances possible. Inevitably there will be exceptions.

- **Our findings may not be politically correct, but we try to be true to the evidence**. As a newspaper columnist on women's issues, Shaunti sometimes receives e-mails from women complaining that she is doing exactly what we intend to do in this book—making generalizations about women. Add the fact that I, as a *guy*, am daring to make those generalizations, and we recognize the potential for controversy. We don't quite know how to get around that, so we decided to just report what we learned. (For any woman sneaking a peak: We do not intend to be offensive; we just want to speak frankly to men, from a man's viewpoint, about *you*. Our sole intention is to help your man understand and love you better. Even if we have to poke fun at the male preoccupation with sex to do it.)

We decided to just report what we learned.

The Thing to Do Next

We think in the pages ahead you're going to receive a lot of very promising invitations to try some new things. Most are incredibly simple, but they may not come naturally. At least at first. Of course, if all you read about here is already instinctive to you, you wouldn't be troubled by randomness, confusion, frustration…and did I mention swamps?

My encouragement to you: Give the process time as you retrain years of incorrect assumptions and counterproductive reactions. Bring a humble attitude. Be willing to practice. Believe it can be done.

Because I've learned that it can be. After several months of being the embedded male, I was watching a movie with Shaunti one night. Halfway through, I casually mentioned that I didn't like the way one female character treated another. Shaunti sat up on the couch, grinned, and said, "You're thinking like a girl!"

Now, she meant it as high praise, but in the small Midwest town where I grew up, that kind of talk could get a guy slugged. But then I realized: Maybe I *had* learned a valuable thing or two about the female universe, just by listening in.

Here's hoping that you do, too.

Intro

Chapter 2

THE DEAL IS NEVER CLOSED

Why her "I do" will always mean "Do you?"—and what to do about it

> Even if your relationship is great, your mate likely has a fundamental insecurity about your love— and when that insecurity is triggered, she may respond in ways that confuse or dismay you until she feels reassured that you love her.

Reassurance

Think of the deals you've struck in your life. Your first car. Your first real job. Your first house. You saw what you wanted, did what you had to do to get it—and you came home with a done deal.

No deal compares to winning a wife, though. You pursued her with all the creativity and resources you could muster, and the deal was done. Your wedding day was the day you proved your love to the world, and to her. Divorce stats to the contrary, I'd bet—since you're reading this book—your marriage feels like the most obviously *closed deal* in your whole life.

Right?

Well, not exactly. As we'll explain in this chapter, it just feels closed for you.

No, your wife isn't still out looking for other suitors. But in an unusual and powerful way that married men don't really understand, your wife doesn't feel permanently loved once the marriage papers are signed. Yes, she *knows* you love her, but there are periodic times when her *feelings* need to be convinced and reassured.

The Truth About "I Do"

It's no surprise that women need to feel loved. What is a surprise is that buried inside most women—even those in great relationships—is a latent insecurity about whether their man *really* loves them, and whether the relationship is okay. This sense of vulnerability may usually be under the surface of their minds, but when it is triggered, most women show signs of distress until the concern is resolved.

You can read "show signs of distress" as "drive their man nuts" if you want.

> Buried inside most women—even those in great relationships—is a latent insecurity about whether their man *really* loves them.

Fact is, you're going to see, as I did, that many of the things that perplex or even anger us about our wife or girl-friend are *signals that they are feeling insecure about our love* or the relationship.

For example, have you ever wondered why your wife:

- asks, "Do you love me?" even though you've done nothing to indicate you've changed your mind about loving her? (In fact, you just told her you loved her this morning on the way out the door!)
- takes your need for space or "cave" time as an indication that you're upset with and trying to get away from her?
- wants to talk, talk, talk about your relationship— especially at the times you *least* want to?
- seems to turn critical or pushy for no reason you can figure?

Reassurance

- gets crabby or "excessively emotional" and seems to push you away—but is unhappy or angry when you *stay* away?

If you're like me, you react to these seemingly unrelated behaviors with confusion and frustration. You become convinced you'll never know what she wants, and could never please her if you did.

But our research for *For Men Only* has persuaded me that every single one of those behaviors is related, and many are easy to resolve. Once you're clued in, you'll see those "drive you nuts" behaviors as red warning lights signaling a breach in your wife's confidence about whether you really love her.

> You'll see those "drive you nuts" behaviors as red warning lights signaling a breach in your wife's confidence about whether you really love her.

I know it sounds crazy to you that your wife might ever wonder whether you love her. But as it turns out, your "I do" actually *didn't* bring permanent emotional closure and put her mind at rest about your feelings for her forever. For her, your "I do" doesn't erase that insecurity about your love that lives under the surface in even the most happily married woman—an insecurity that, when triggered, becomes a deeply felt uncertainty: "Do you? Do you *still*…love me? Are we still okay?"

Now, you might be thinking, "Surely this doesn't apply to my wife! She *knows* I love her!" Yes, she probably does. But we're not talking here about what she *knows logically*, but rather about the *feeling* that rises up when something has triggered it. Even otherwise secure, confident wives find that this latent "Does he really love me?" insecurity is relatively easily triggered—and it is this feeling that we need to take seriously.

Having gotten so much input from women, I now believe that if men can get clarity on this hidden insecurity, we'll experience a lot more understanding, peace, and pleasure at home.

Let's begin with looking closer at the mystery.

Three Surprises (What "Never a Done Deal" Feels Like to Her)

As the token embedded male for our surveys and focus groups, I was in for a number of big surprises on the subject of women's relational, triggered insecurity.

My First Surprise—How frequent these feelings are

Whereas most guys coast along rarely thinking about the health of the relationship, for most women that is unthinkable.

Seven out of every ten women said their relationship and how their man felt about them was anywhere from "occasionally" to nearly always on their minds. Fewer than 20 percent said that they wondered about it only when things were difficult. Just 12 percent never thought about it.

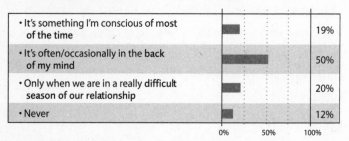

Under what circumstances do you think about your relationship, whether it is going well, or how your husband/significant other feels about you? [Choose One Answer]

• It's something I'm conscious of most of the time	19%
• It's often/occasionally in the back of my mind	50%
• Only when we are in a really difficult season of our relationship	20%
• Never	12%

*Because of rounding, totals slightly exceed 100%.

I'm guessing that for most guys, "occasional" thoughts about the closeness of our relationship might boil down to birthdays, anniversaries, and when something goes drastically, obviously haywire. But when we asked women what they meant by "occasional" concern about how their man felt about them, I often heard that it meant several times a week, or *whenever it was triggered* (such as by what we might consider a relatively minor spat).

We checked these results by asking the question another way and got an even stronger response. Four out of five women acknowledged sometimes feeling insecure about their man's love and the relationship. Among women under forty-five, the percentage jumped to 91 percent, and among those with children in middle school or younger, it was almost universal.

I realize us guys can understand this foreign-seeming insecurity if we compare it to one of our own. As one woman put it, "You know that record that's always running in a guy's head about providing? Well, *we* have the same fundamental concern about our relationship all the time. And if it's not going well, it can mess up everything else in our lives."

My Second Surprise—How intensely painful these feelings are

Almost every woman I asked said she cared about her man so much that when this relational insecurity was triggered, it was very painful—sometimes almost debilitating—and it became difficult, if not impossible, for them to get it off their

Reassurance

minds. As several women put it, "When we're at odds, nothing is right with the world until it is resolved."

On the survey, three out of four women agreed, saying that this "Does he really love me?" concern left them feeling preoccupied, emotionally withdrawn, depressed, or affected in other "visible" ways. Look at the data:

When you are feeling insecure about his love or the relationship, which of the following are true <u>about your feelings</u>? [Choose all correct answers.*]

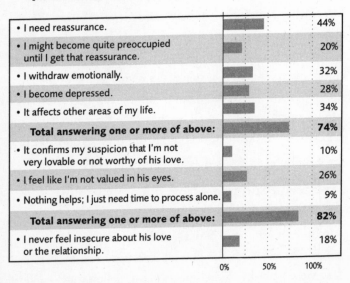

• I need reassurance.	44%
• I might become quite preoccupied until I get that reassurance.	20%
• I withdraw emotionally.	32%
• I become depressed.	28%
• It affects other areas of my life.	34%
Total answering one or more of above:	**74%**
• It confirms my suspicion that I'm not very lovable or not worthy of his love.	10%
• I feel like I'm not valued in his eyes.	26%
• Nothing helps; I just need time to process alone.	9%
Total answering one or more of above:	**82%**
• I never feel insecure about his love or the relationship.	18%

0%   50%   100%

* Because respondents could choose more than one answer, results do not add up to 100%.

You and I have every right to think the woman we love *shouldn't* feel insecure. We're faithful, we go to work, we *do* love her…and we're still here. But just because we think our wife *should* feel secure doesn't mean that she always *does*. Which leads to my third realization.

> Just because we think our wife *should* feel secure about our love doesn't mean that she always *does*.

My Third Surprise—How resistant to "logic" (i.e. my logic) her feelings remain

As Shaunti points out: "It's irrelevant whether she should 'know logically' that she's loved. If she doesn't *feel* loved, it's the same for her as if she *isn't* loved."

One survey taker put it this way:

> I wish he realized that where he processes everything based just on logic, I process information based also on emotion. He says that I know logically that he loves me, and that should be enough. But the fact is, emotionally I don't *feel* loved.

Again, think about one of our own "resistant to logic" concerns. Even secure guys who are good at their jobs inwardly feel—all logic to the contrary—that they still could be just a few mistakes or industry hiccups away from losing their job. And even women in good relationships feel that they could be just a few bad blowups away from losing their man's love.

As one woman said, "I don't think we ever take his love for granted."

> Even women in good relationships feel that they could be just a few bad blowups away from losing their man's love.

Hidden Triggers

What sets these insecurity tremors off? What in the course of everyday life in a reasonably healthy relationship is most likely to drive her to wonder, "Does he still love me?" (Other than the big, obvious factors such as infidelity or physical violence?) Here are a few triggers:

- **Conflict**—anything that gives her the feeling that something is wrong, that the two of you are at odds, or that you are unhappy with her. As one woman put it, "A lot of desperate feelings surface for me when I feel like my husband is displeased with me. I know it sounds old-fashioned, and I'm a pretty independent person, but it still really affects me."

- **Withdrawal**—which is, of course, how we often respond to conflict! We tend to retreat into silence to escape unwanted feelings, because we can't fully articulate something yet, or to avoid saying something hurtful. Unfortunately, seeing her man withdraw or be moody usually generates *more* unwanted feelings for a woman! Several women described the resulting thought this way: "What happens if he doesn't snap out of it this time?!"

- **Silence**—even if nothing's wrong. Because women have a radar for *unspoken* conflict, it's pretty easy for women to jump to conclusions when their man is more withdrawn or quiet than usual. As one woman put it, "If you're quiet, it must be me." When that happens, see it for what it is and instead of getting defensive ("Why do you always assume there's something wrong?!"), use it as an opportunity to reassure her of your love.

- **Her "emotional bank account" is depleted**— perhaps she's exhausted, or her work or the children have been particularly taxing. This may even have nothing to do with you...but she could be more easily "triggered" if her emotional bank account has nothing left in it.

Reassurance

- **You're absent a lot**—even if you hate the obligations that keep you away, she's more likely to experience your absence as a challenge to her security in your love. (See chapter 4 for more on creating "security.")

- **Unresolved relationship issues**—a trigger that most guys miss entirely. If a woman has a concern about the relationship that doesn't feel "resolved"—even if there's no conflict involved—she is going to want to talk. And if we try to avoid it, it only makes her insecurity—and her desire to talk—worse.

Once we recognize these triggers and see the red warning light for what it is—a signal that she needs to be reassured of our love—we can take some incredibly simple steps toward being part of the answer for her, rather than part of the problem.

A Practical Guide to Turning Off the Red Warning Light

I hope you're seeing by now that a woman is likely to experience an undercurrent of emotional insecurity in her relationship *even if* you and I are totally innocent of intent, injury, or error (not that we always *are*, but work with me here). But that doesn't mean we can't be part of the solution.

Maybe a husband's responsibility and opportunity in this regard is what the apostle Paul had in mind when he wrote the simple admonition "Husbands, love your wives..." in his letter to the church at Ephesus. I don't hear any echoes of "The deal is sealed" in his words. Or "Once you've won a wife, Bubba, you're off the hook." What I hear is much more dynamic: *love, go on loving, continue to prove your love, keep on winning her heart with your love...*

> I don't hear any echoes of "Once you've won a wife, Bubba, you're off the hook."

Reassurance

So how do you and I address the fact that our wife carries around this fundamental insecurity about our love? Based on all the research, there are two key solutions:

1) In the face of insecurity, reassure her.
2) Even after you've caught her, continue to pursue her.

Thankfully, both are completely doable for ordinary guys like you and me.

Part 1. Regular Reassurance

Once her insecurity has been triggered and her heart is wondering, "Does he really love me?" the solution is simple: Reassure her that you do. Here are five ways to do that.

1. *During conflict, reassure her of your love.*

During the disagreement, the misunderstanding, the really bad treatment? Yes. In the middle of a conflict, affirm your love as real and enduring, quite separate from your anger or her behavior.

That is the magic bullet that almost every woman told us would make all the difference: If their man would say, "I'm angry right now, and I need some space, but *I want you to know that we're okay.*" On the survey, a whopping 95 percent of women said that this one step on our part would diminish or even eliminate the emotional turmoil on their part.

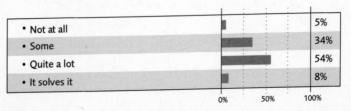

In an emotional conflict, if your husband/significant other initiates a step to reassure you of his love, how much does it help diminish any turmoil you are feeling? [Choose one answer.]

• Not at all	5%
• Some	34%
• Quite a lot	54%
• It solves it	8%

0%   50%   100%

*Because of rounding, results slightly exceed 100%.

That is the magic bullet that almost every woman told us would make all the difference.

Chances are, in conflict, your woman is feeling unloved (even unlovable) and needs you to look her in the eye and tell her that you love her and you're not going anywhere.

Okay, reality check: You won't *feel* your words in the same way you did when you were parked above the city in your convertible and her perfume was driving you crazy. It's one thing for us to give reassurances when things are peachy, but quite another when we're at odds with each other and we'd rather stomp out to the garage and split a block of wood with our bare hands.

But the survey also showed that 86 percent of women said that bolstered by our "I want you to know that we're okay" reassurance, they'd be better able to give us the space we need. (Do you see the possibilities? Reassure her of your love, *then* stomp out to the garage!) Why? Because we've reassured them on the original question, *Does he still love me?*

It's one thing for us to give reassurances when things are peachy, but quite another when we're at odds and would rather stomp out to the garage and split a block of wood with our bare hands.

Reassurance

Suppose you and your husband/significant other are in the middle of an emotional conflict, and he eventually says, "I don't want to talk about this right now." If he were to add a reassurance, such as, "I want you to know that we're okay," would that make you more or less likely to be able to give him space? [Choose One Answer]

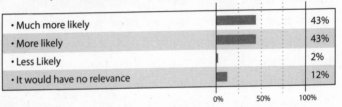

• Much more likely	43%
• More likely	43%
• Less Likely	2%
• It would have no relevance	12%

0%   50%   100%

There is one final step to making this magic bullet really work, though. After you've had your space "for a while," you have to come back and be willing to address the original issue, without making her bring it up.

Easy? No. Effective? You bet. Because, as one woman said, "The fact that he comes back often matters more than the reason for the conflict in the first place."

> "The fact that he comes back often matters more than the reason for the conflict in the first place."

2. When you need space, reassure her that it's not about her.

If you're like most guys, when you have a lot of thinking to do—even if there's no conflict—you need time alone to process things. Most women we heard from react exactly the opposite—only 9 percent wanted to handle their feelings of insecurity alone. (Which is also why, when you two are at odds and you most want to get away to process in silence, she most wants to talk.)

So state your need in the context of hers: "Honey, right now I just need some time alone—I'm just out of sorts. It has nothing to do with how I feel about you." That will make it much easier for her to let you have space without misinterpreting your need.

3. If she's upset, realize she doesn't need space— she needs a hug.

When our wife or girlfriend is upset, we do what we would do with other guys: We give her space to work things out. But with very few exceptions, when women are upset they don't want space. They want a hug.

I think this next comment is one of the most valuable "just do this" quotes in the book:

Reassurance

All I want is him to know that half the time I'm just as confused as he is. Instead of getting upset and leaving me alone to "calm down," I just want him to come close and give me a huge hug and let me know he loves me and he wants me to feel better again.

4. If she needs to talk about the relationship, do your best to listen without becoming defensive.

The next step is a little bit more intimidating, but essential. If she *does* need to talk, try to see it as she does: a joint problem-solving session instead of an attack on *you*.

"When I tell him how I feel about something concerning our relationship, I am just trying to share my feelings so we can discuss it," one woman told us. "But he takes it as criticism, and then I feel like the bad guy for bringing it up. I wish he could understand that it's important for me to be able to talk about these things and understand that I'm not just being critical."

All this research has convinced me that when most women bring up a problem, they are *not* thinking that we've failed—and we need to push through our natural tendency to view what they are saying as criticism.

5. If she is being difficult, don't stop—keep reassuring her of your love.

Finally, let's address a dynamic that confuses and even aggravates us: the importance of reassuring and showing love to our wife *even when* she's difficult, resistant, or pushing us away. As you can probably guess by now, that is usually just one more (and more difficult!) sign of that "Do you really love me?" question.

When we asked some women why they might push their husband away or make it hard for their husband to love them (by being difficult or critical, for example), most women knew exactly what we were talking about. But they had a hard time explaining *why* they did it. It was really, they said, a subconscious attempt to assuage their inner uncertainty about his love.

Another woman made this comment, which is long, but very valuable for confused men like you and me:

> You have to realize, if a woman says, "I need to hear that you love me," and the guy dutifully says, "I love you," well, that's essentially meaningless: like she made him say something he didn't feel. So if she's feeling confused and neglected and really does want to be assured of his feelings, she can't just ask. And if they are at odds, she's maybe a little mad at him,

so when he approaches her, she pushes him away *even though that is what she most wants*! But if he'll put aside his pride and try again, if he'll risk grabbing her hand and saying something like "Don't go away. I want to know what's wrong," that will break through her defenses. It tells her that no matter how she's feeling right then, that *whew*, he really loves her.

Fair warning: This will include times where we've sensed insecurity and are trying to reassure her—and still get pushed away. Few things drive a guy crazy more than the sense of being tested or manipulated, and most of us soon give up in disgust. I can't tell you how many times when facing resistance I've thought, *Fine, suit yourself. I've got to go cut the lawn anyway.* And then I pretty much put the incident out of my mind. Unfortunately, she can't.

She's still seeking the answer to the original question: "Do you still love me?"*

My advice is, if you're speechless with frustration at that point, you're still in the game. Forget giving speeches and simply reach for her.

> If you're speechless with frustration at that point, forget giving speeches and simply reach for her.

* This topic—including how we can see even complaining or criticizing as signals of "I want your love!"—is developed much more in Emerson Eggerichs's book *Love and Respect*.

Part 2. Persistent Pursuit

Now we come to an even more valuable tool for a man who wants to show his wife that he still means his "I do": pursuit. It's even better than saying those reassuring words once she's already feeling insecure. Pursuit is action—it's what you did when you first saw her and wanted to make her yours. It *prevents* a lot of her insecurity. It fills up her emotional bank account. And pursuit is what she still deeply desires and needs in her marriage, even if us "close the deal" kind of guys are already on to the next big deal—completing our education, launching a career, raising kids, perfecting our golf swing...

All worthy goals, mind you. But they tend to make us forget that the pursuit of her that we thought was completed really isn't.

Pursuit *prevents* a lot of her insecurity.

One woman we interviewed recounted a common story line that captures the dilemma perfectly:

> I know a woman who was divorced for quite a few years, but then this new guy started pursuing her. At first she was cautious—she was fine on her own and didn't think he was her "type." But he just *wooed* her—there's no other way of putting it. He was very

Reassurance

attentive, and made it clear that he thought she was something special and that he wouldn't be dissuaded that easily. He sent her flowers all the time, which is one of her "things," and dropped her little notes, and it just made her feel so special. As he pursued her steadily like that for several years, she saw all his terrific qualities and fell hard in love. They got married—and almost immediately she began to think that something was wrong. All those little things that said "I love you" to her—well, he stopped doing them! No more flowers or notes or pursuing. It seemed to her like once they got married, he suddenly stopped caring about her. And now, he doesn't understand why she's upset. He just says, "Of *course* I love you, honey!" And then goes on about his day. Meantime, he doesn't realize that his wife is getting seriously, seriously depressed.

Of course, you and I can identify with this story from the guy's side. It's common for men to think that pursuing goes with dating, not with marriage. But women don't see things that way. There is never that magic moment of closure, when they feel permanently, fully, deeply loved. *They think that's what the rest of married life is for!* That's why they need and deserve to be pursued every day.

In fact, several women compared the need to feel pursued by their husbands with the need that a man has to feel sexually desired by his wife! If it's that important, what is a smart married man to do?

Big-screen answer: Give chase.

Pixel answer: Ask yourself, *What did I do when I was dating that made me so pickin' irresistible?*

> Ask yourself, *What did I do when I was dating that made me so pickin' irresistible?*

Probably you spent hours just hanging out together. You listened. You flirted. You sent little e-mails during the day just to say hi. You shared dreams.

You said things like:

"We're so good together."

"I can't imagine life without you."

"I'm so glad God brought us together."

"I love you so much it hurts…"

You proved to her, in other words, that you were smitten.

Want a portrait of pursuit in marriage? You and I should consider that we might already be masters of it. Now that we know the chase isn't over, we just need to remember to do what came so naturally before.

Reassurance

"You didn't come after me."

Maybe you remember the 1998 remake of the old Disney movie *The Parent Trap*, starring Dennis Quaid, Natasha Richardson, and then-twelve-year-old Lindsay Lohan. Our young daughter loves this movie, and we were watching it for the twentieth time one night when Shaunti pointed out a perfect illustration for this book. In the movie, two preteen girls realize they are twins, separated at birth when their parents divorced—so they plot to get them back together by switching places. The British mom and American dad still care about each other, and when they finally meet again, Nick asks his ex-wife, Elizabeth, about what happened between them.

Nick: It ended so fast.... So...about the day you packed.... Why did you do it?

Elizabeth: Nick, we were so young, and we each had tempers. We each said foolish things. So I packed, got on my first 747 and...you didn't come after me.

(Dead silence.)

Nick: I didn't know I was supposed to.

Elizabeth: (Smiling bravely) Well, it really doesn't matter now.... So let's just put on a good face for the girls, shall we, and get this show on the road.

Shaunti said this was an example of where the woman really *wanted* him to come after her.

I asked, "But why didn't she just *tell* him that she wanted him to stop her from leaving? Why play games and make him read her mind?"

She looked at me, totally astonished. "Because if she said, 'Come after me,' it wouldn't *mean* anything! It would be her decision, not his. She'd always doubt whether he did it on his own or because she asked him and guilted him into it."

Oh. Now I get it.

The movie, by the way, ends well. Nick finally realizes that in spite of Elizabeth's seeming to push him away, she wanted him to follow. And so he does. Because he learns to pursue, learns to reassure, the family is reunited.

Chances are, your wife or girlfriend is carrying around an unseen uncertainty about your love and needs you to come after her, too, look her in the eye, and tell her that you love her…and you're not going to let her get away.

Reassurance

Chapter  **3**

WINDOWS...OPEN!

What you should know about the fabulous female brain (a guide for lower life forms)

> *Women deal with multiple thoughts and emotions from their past and present all the time, at the same time—and these can't be easily dismissed.*

ne day early on in our research, my kids and I dropped by the home of some close friends, Alec and Susie. While our children went outside to play, Alec asked me what I'd been learning about the mysterious other gender. I tried to describe a growing realization: The female brain is not a normal instrument.

Normal, Alec and I agreed, would mean "male." Instead, I described what many women had told me: that their thought lives were almost like busy computers with multiple

Emotions

51

windows open and running all at once, unwanted pop-ups intruding all the time, and little ability to close out or ignore any of that mental or emotional activity until a more convenient time.

My friend shook his head in amazement. Strange, we both agreed. Very strange.

> Their thought lives are almost like busy computers with multiple windows open and running all at once.

Susie, sitting at her computer nearby, had been listening, much amused, to the male sleuths at work in her kitchen. So my friend and I decided to test my working conclusions on the spot. "Okay, hon," said Alec, "so what is in your brain *right now?*"

She looked up. "Right now? Well, let's see." She started ticking things off on her fingers. "I'm thinking about all the points I want to make in this article I'm writing. I'm thinking I need to check the pizza in the oven pretty soon. I'm hoping the kids are doing okay out on the trampoline and thinking I should go check on them. I'm wondering whether we're going to hear back tonight on this business deal we're waiting on and thinking about what I can say to move things forward." She hesitated a moment, then looked up at Alec. "And if you really want to know, I keep worrying about the argument you and I had this morning, and whether you're still upset."

We looked stunned. "There's probably more," she said. "You want me to keep going?"

Alec verbalized what any guy would be wondering: "How do you get anything done with all that stuff in your head?" And more to the point, "Why don't you just turn off all the other thoughts so you can concentrate?"

Susie looked perplexed. "Because I can't," she said. "And even if I did, they'd come back."

After hearing this sort of thing dozens of times, I realized that how a woman multitasks her thoughts and feelings isn't just an interesting academic difference between the sexes. It probably impacts how your wife or girlfriend relates to you every single day. That means a closer look at this mysterious mental difference is definitely in order.

> This female multitasking of thoughts and feelings impacts how your wife or girlfriend relates to you every single day.

Her Mysterious Matrix

Picture this: You're on your computer, moving between six or seven open screens on your desktop. Perhaps you're juggling three or four Word documents, an Excel spreadsheet or two, and your home budgeting program. In addition, your e-mail program and Internet browser are running, and your computer is playing your favorite Webcast radio program. It's a digital Grand Central Station.

Now add another dimension: Imagine that some of the open files and programs are actually weeks old and have been running there in the background the whole time. Even worse, your computer is infected with spyware that keeps causing annoying advertisements to pop up. You've tried to close these unwanted files and pop-ups many times. You've installed anti-spyware programs and rebooted your computer. But those pesky things just keep coming back. The best you can do is to minimize or ignore them so you can focus on the other half-dozen tasks you're actively juggling at any one time...

Welcome to a woman's mental and emotional world—a world that has probably affected yours more than you realize. Here's what our surveys found:

- First, most women juggle multiple thoughts and feelings at the same time.
- Second, about half of all women have stored thoughts or feelings from the past that regularly pop up into active mode *whether they want them to or not*.

- Third, women seem consistently unable to close these windows as easily as men can.

Let's look more carefully at what each of these statements means, how this affects you, and how to make the most of the mysterious but wonderful way she's wired.

> Women seem consistently unable to close these windows as easily as men can.

Of course, to make any progress on this discussion, we'll have to switch to male-pattern processing. That would mean, for example, taking one thing at a time.

There's Lots Goin' On in There

Take multitasking: I've suggested that like a computer running multiple tasks, my wife will tend to have many different thoughts and feelings all running in her brain at the same time. Where I would tend to process thoughts and feelings sequentially—working on one screen at a time, closing it, and moving on to the next—Shaunti is likely to have many screens open simultaneously and is able to jump back and forth between them at will. Or against her will.

Emotions

In fact, on the survey nearly eight of ten women described themselves in very similar ways. Agreement became almost universal (in the 90–95 percent range) for women under forty-five and those with middle-school or younger children at home.

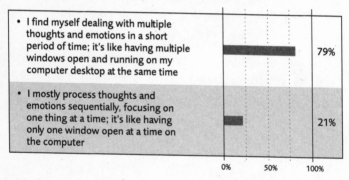

Which scenario best describes how you experience thoughts and emotions? [Choose One Answer]

- I find myself dealing with multiple thoughts and emotions in a short period of time; it's like having multiple windows open and running on my computer desktop at the same time — 79%
- I mostly process thoughts and emotions sequentially, focusing on one thing at a time; it's like having only one window open at a time on the computer — 21%

This may perplex us, but think how the unique properties of the female brain prepare her in so many ways for success. Think, for example, of how you've watched in amazement as your wife or mom managed an onslaught of cranky kids, made dinner, talked on the phone to a colleague, and let the cat out...all at the same time. Think of how your wife or girlfriend's brain has nurtured countless relationships or deftly managed the web of commitments in an extended family while holding down a job. You get the idea.

Most men are very different. Early in our marriage, if Shaunti found me sitting by myself, she'd ask me what I was thinking. When I answered "nothing," she'd get irritated and press me to *please* tell her what I was thinking. She didn't understand that I really was thinking...nothing! My desktop was empty, a screen saver was up, and no one was home.

Do you relate? Women don't. As one woman put it: "There's never a time that there's nothing going on in my head. If I answer 'nothing,' it's because I'm mad at him!"

> "There's never a time that there's nothing going on in my head."

This female matrix of multiple emotions and thoughts—all running at the same time—helps to explain some perplexing things, including:

- *Why women jump topics in the middle of conversation.* When this happens, we might think: a) she's going off on a tangent, b) she's muddled, c) she's not paying attention, d) she's not being respectful, or e) all of the above. But then we only have one window open, so we're only having one conversation. Turns out she's already

Emotions

deep into, oh, five or six at the same time! We just didn't know it.

- *Why your wife or girlfriend, by comparison, often has so much more than you to talk about at the end of the day.* Now you know—even at the end of a very busy day, you've only been busy running down *one* track! But not her.

Invasion of the Pop-Ups

Not only do women have multiple thoughts running at once, about half regularly experience uninvited thoughts or feelings—from the present or the past—that pop up and interrupt their day. For the men who live with them, that means that they often interrupt ours, too!

More than a man, a woman will be regularly hit by unresolved emotional issues or hurts from a conversation or concern from last night, last month, or ten years ago. To the man in her life, it might seem that her past keeps crowding into her present, that she's choosing to dwell on something that's better left alone, or that she's choosing to irrationally rehash or return to a matter that he thought was closed. But for her it's not irrational—in fact, if this is the way she's wired, it would be irrational for her *not* to address something that has circled back around.

According to our national survey, about half of all women are interrupted by these pop-up thoughts or feelings multiple times a week, even multiple times a day. Among younger women and those with children at home, the proportion again was higher—at between 55–60 percent of survey takers. Perhaps not surprisingly, the percentage rose as high as 80 percent among women who described their relationship as shaky and those in difficult financial straits.

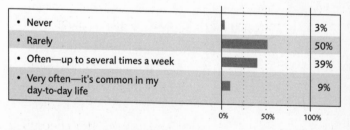

Some women say that emotions from experiences in the recent or even distant past (particularly negative ones) sometimes rise up in their minds. These may be triggered, or may seem to arise from nowhere. How often do you experience this? [Choose One Answer]

• Never	3%
• Rarely	50%
• Often—up to several times a week	39%
• Very often—it's common in my day-to-day life	9%

0%   50%   100%

Emotions

*Due to rounding, total slightly exceeds 100%.

It's not that women are helpless victims of these mental and emotional intruders. They're just more likely to have them, and to have difficulty getting rid of them, than men. One woman in a focus group put it this way: "A lot of women will say, 'Don't play that tape in your head. You have to stop. Stop, don't go there with that thought.' It's easier said than done, but at least we try."

Actually, we do this, too...

Does that comment sound startlingly familiar to you? I realized that we men can understand this struggle intimately because we have a visual parallel. Every man knows what it is like to have tempting images pop up in his brain, unwanted…just like our wives have strong emotional memories or concerns pop up, unwanted. As one woman wrote in:

> If all men are truly visual and can't help it, then I think they should please understand that women are truly verbal and can't help it. For example, the things men say to us are in mental tape archives and are as real today as they were the moment they were spoken.

"The things men say to us are in mental tape archives and are as real today as they were the moment they were spoken."

So that's why...

The involuntary, long-term nature of this can help explain why more than one husband has felt:

- blindsided when his wife brings up something that happened two years ago;
- surprised by a sudden flare-up of emotion attached to a memory;
- stung by unexpected heat that turns a conversation into an argument; or
- dismayed that she got hurt by something seemingly outside of the moment's mood or context.

If you're like me, you might think that she is unwilling to "let go" of something—an old offense or memory or grudge. That she's choosing an "emotional" response, instead of a "rational" one—as if the two were mutually exclusive. (Hint: For women, they're not.) What's more likely is that her past is emotionally invading her present, and her current reaction is a quite reasonable response to the fact that *she* is feeling blindsided, surprised, stung, or dismayed by the current experience of an old problem that has never really been resolved or healed. Or perhaps there's some current trouble that keeps invading her awareness—an open, running window that keeps painfully popping to the fore, even if she doesn't want it there.

Emotions

> ▽If her past is emotionally invading her present, her emotional reaction is a reasonable response.

Where's the "Close" Button?

And that brings us to the most important piece of this dynamic: that most women find it difficult or impossible to close out and ignore unwanted thoughts and feelings. We've all heard that women don't "compartmentalize" like we do, but I never before understood what that meant.

To illustrate, let's go back to that conversation in our friends' kitchen. I, too, had several things on my mind—including that I should check on the kids out in the backyard. But when I compared notes with Shaunti, we realized that I could handle those thoughts much differently than she could have in the same situation:

Jeff: I'm talking with Alec, and think, "Should I check on the kids? Yeah, I'll do that in about five minutes." Then I simply put it out of my mind—like on a five-minute mental timer. I don't give it another thought until the timer goes off.

Shaunti: How do you *do* that? I would love to put a thought on a timer and not think about it, but it's impossible. I simply have to function around that awareness that the kids need to be checked on or my friend is having a hard time with her marriage and needs me to call her or whatever. It never really goes away until the issue is resolved.

Of course, when I told Shaunti my timer function could actually put an issue that I didn't want to deal with on hold and out of mind *for weeks,* her interest in my brain turned to alarm.

Our survey shows that the vast majority of women just aren't wired to easily ignore unwanted thoughts. As one woman said: "The best I can do is to 'minimize' the other windows, not close them. I'm not actively thinking about those things every minute, but they aren't gone, either. And they often pop back up and become active when I don't want them to."

The vast majority of women just aren't wired to easily ignore unwanted thoughts.

Emotions

On those occasions when you have multiple emotional "windows" open, how readily can you usually dismiss negative thoughts and emotions that are bothering you? [Choose One Answer]

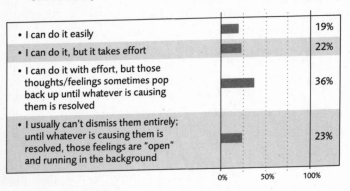

• I can do it easily	19%
• I can do it, but it takes effort	22%
• I can do it with effort, but those thoughts/feelings sometimes pop back up until whatever is causing them is resolved	36%
• I usually can't dismiss them entirely; until whatever is causing them is resolved, those feelings are "open" and running in the background	23%

For more than four out of five, closing out their unwanted thoughts either required effort or was impossible. (For women under age forty-five, the number rose to almost 90 percent.) The vast majority indicated that those thoughts would never really go away, or would at least keep returning, until whatever was causing them was resolved.

Which means that our usual manly advice to "Just don't think about it" is about as helpful as another shovelful of sand in the Sahara.

We Can Relate

Here's a way that you can almost certainly relate to what this feels like. Imagine that your company just lost its biggest client, and at 5:00 p.m. on Friday your boss says, "I'll need to see you in my office first thing Monday morning." If you're like me, your weekend is ruined, and anxious thoughts wreak havoc until Monday arrives. Your normal ability to compartmentalize is compromised by the magnitude of the concern.

Women aren't that dissimilar—it's just that their magnitude threshold is far lower than ours. Just as you couldn't close out the anxious thoughts about what might happen on Monday, she can't close out all sorts of open windows.

That gives you a bit of a glimpse into how your wife feels when you have a bad argument in the morning and are at odds with each other. You can usually go off to work and put it out of your mind, but she may be completely unable to. The awareness that something is wrong is stalking her thoughts all day, until the argument is resolved and she is reassured.

> You can usually go off to work and put an argument out of your mind, but she may be completely unable to.

Emotions

Real-Life Example

I think we men need to have our eyes opened to the real-life examples that are all around us so we can see how this actually works and what to *do* about it. So let me pick an example that just happened last night. Shaunti was out of town with the kids, and a colleague invited me over for dinner with his wife, Donna, and two small children. When I arrived, Bob was working in another room with one of those fire-starter devices that you click to get a flame. The following conversation occurred as the adults sat down for dinner a few minutes later:

Donna: Honey, what did you do with the fire-starter?

Bob: I left it in the other room.

Donna: But...the kids are in there.

Bob: It's okay. It would be impossible for them to figure out how to get a flame—it's pretty difficult to use.

Donna: But what if—

Bob: Really, hon, there's no way they would be strong enough to click the flame on.

Donna: Okay...That's true....

Previously, I wouldn't have thought a thing about this conversation. But now, as I watched Donna across the table, I could tell—with my newly acquired, supersensitive male radar—that a window had popped open and was not going to close until something set her mind at ease. So I mentioned to Bob and Donna what I'd been learning about how women couldn't usually just *decide* to close a window and not think about something that was bothering them.

Donna sat bolt upright. "That's it!" she said, "That's exactly what I'm feeling." She pushed away from the table, moved the fire-starter out of the kids' reach, and came back.

"Now," she said, "I can enjoy dinner."

Bob and I both realized that if she hadn't been encouraged to take that ten-second action, she would have been distracted and unable to truly relax and enjoy the next hour of dinner. Even though she acknowledged that Bob was almost certainly correct that the kids couldn't engage the fire-starter, the window would have been open and bugging her.

> If she hadn't been encouraged to "close that window," she would have been unable to relax and enjoy dinner.

I hope you see all sorts of ramifications of this female wiring. It explains:

Emotions

- *Why she seems preoccupied by "little things"*—even if you tell her to just ignore them.
- *Why she seems to have been "stewing" over an argument*—or seems (to your male mind) to feel overly insecure about a disagreement you'd already dismissed or forgotten.
- *Why she might be too tired or upset for sex.* One woman put it this way: "Try to understand—we're carrying around a *lot* that we need to get out of our heads before we can really even feel like sex."

I don't know about you, but I don't even *need* my head to feel like sex.

Sequential Strategies for Sequential Minds

What's the average taken-aback man to do?

The good news of this chapter, and this book, is that a little understanding can go a very long way. Based on our research—and on my personal experience—I recommend three positive responses:

1. Rethink your assumptions about how *she* thinks.

For example, consider: Maybe she's *not* trying to hassle you by wanting to talk about fourteen things as soon as you come through the door after work. She really does have fourteen files open and running. And she can't just "not think about something" that may be unresolved from the morning.

Also, if she brings up old wounds, she may not be holding on to a grudge, but actually trying to process through it so she can resolve it, close the window, and let it go.

> She may not be holding on to a grudge, but actually trying to process through it so she can let it go.

In any of these cases, you can help by letting her—actually encouraging her—to process these things the way she probably needs to: by talking it through and having you listen (see chapter 5 on listening). (Note to self: If I'm smart, I'll ask what her day was like well before bedtime.)

2. Realize you may not *be* the issue, even though you're affected by the issue.

Well, okay, it's *possible* you're the problem. But more likely, now that you're aware of all the traffic streaming through her

Emotions

consciousness, you can see why you shouldn't just jump to the usual conclusion of, *Uh-oh, she thinks I did something wrong again.*

(Pointer from Shaunti—If you're not sure whether you're the problem, or whether you just happen to be around when the problem comes up, *ask.* Something like, "Sweetheart, did I do something wrong, or are you upset about something else?")

3. Be her hero and help her clear those distracting or painful windows so they don't keep coming back.

Most important, remember that because it's harder for her to just push something out of her mind, there's more of a risk that she'll be living in a marginally unhappy state for hours or days if something is wrong. Thankfully, you can have an important part in resolving it.

Let's say a pop-up of some old hurt has arisen involuntarily, and she's having trouble closing it. Maybe she's unable to get a conflict with her boss off her mind or an old hurt from something you said has risen up in her head. Now's the time to step up and give her a listening ear, a hug, or the reassurance she needs (see chapter 2 for how to reassure her) so she can resolve it in her mind.

Realize the futility of telling her, "Just don't think about it," and encourage her if she needs to take some action to close the window.

Even better, take some action yourself. Get up from the dinner table, go get her the fire-starter, and say, "I wanted to be sure you could enjoy dinner without worrying."

Be one of the few, the proud, the in-the-know heroes.

Chapter 4

YOUR REAL JOB IS CLOSER TO HOME

How your provider/protector instinct can leave her feeling more unsafe and less cared for

> *Your woman needs emotional security and closeness with you so much that she will endure financial insecurity to get it.*

It happened the minute I decided that Shaunti was the woman I wanted to marry. As soon as I thought about popping the question and accelerating our relationship into high gear...I stalled.

Most guys I've talked to can relate. All my forward momentum vanished as anxiety stopped me in my tracks. The issue wasn't her or how much I loved her or what I really wanted to happen between us—and soon.

73

The issue was money. It suddenly hit home: "How will I take care of a wife and provide for her financially?" I didn't know much about relationship stuff, but I knew one thing: Women want security.

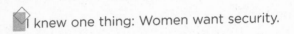

I knew one thing: Women want security.

I grew up in a small farming community in Michigan and had known plenty of financial struggles in my life. After high school I scraped by in the restaurant business for seven years before I went to college. But Shaunti was from the upper-middle-class suburbs of Washington, DC, and hadn't experienced similar struggles. I was concerned about what she would consider a "normal" standard of living and whether I could provide it. So I waited. With that in mind, when I graduated from law school, I took a job with a big New York law firm that included a very good salary.

Finally, I figured, I could provide. So we got married and moved into a doorman building in the heart of Manhattan. In New York, doorman buildings are common but pricey. But Shaunti preferred one because it made her feel more *secure*, she said.

Aha! I thought, confident in my manly insight into her needs. *Even if I might have preferred a different job, I'm doing what men do. I'm providing security for my wife.*

Then I proceeded to work eighty-hour weeks for the next five years to pay for it all. During that time, whenever Shaunti said that I was choosing work over her or that I didn't care about her needs, I experienced a strong and predictable reaction—I got upset. *How can she accuse me of not caring about her when I am busting my tail to prove exactly that!*

Recently, when I asked a friend what he thought it meant that "women want security," he described a common male dilemma: "It means I can't ever stop running," he said. "I need to do whatever I have to do to *ensure* that she doesn't feel financially insecure. And if it means that I have to work really long hours, or stick with a job that I don't like all that much, so be it."

Perhaps you, too, have felt caught between a rock and a hard place, knowing that your wife wants you to provide a nice life for her and the kids, but she also wants you home by dinner. Impossible financial expectations on her part? Maybe, but *probably not*. As you'll see in this chapter, men may be really frustrated by what they think their wives expect—but their wives may have no such expectations. In our case it turns out the doorman building in Manhattan wasn't nearly as important as I'd thought.

Security

Money Talks, but "Emotional Security" Sings

Our research shows that yes, women want security. But they mean something very different by it than we do. When a woman thinks of "security," her primary thought is not about a house, a savings account, or tuition for the kids. For her, "emotional security" matters most: feeling emotionally connected and close to you, and knowing that you are there for her no matter what. Sure, providing financially is appreciated, but for most women it's nowhere near the top of their list.

> When a woman thinks of "security," her primary thought is not about a house, a savings account, or tuition for the kids.

In fact, as one woman told us: "It's not even on the *same* list! Feeling secure and close in the relationship is so much more important, it's not even part of the same discussion as work or money."

Forgive my confusion. Yes, I heard Shaunti *say* she wanted more of me. But I also heard her say that she wanted the doorman building. I assumed that she was choosing financial security over a saner and more enjoyable career for me. Her insistence that she wanted to make changes so I could be around struck me as appreciative gestures aimed at making me feel less pressured.

But now I realize—a little late—that she actually *meant* it.

On the survey, seven out of ten married women said that if they had to, they would rather endure financial struggles than distance in the relationship.

Why don't you read that again. I know we find it impossible, but it's true: 70 percent of married women would prefer to be financially *insecure* than endure a lack of closeness with their husbands.

In fact, even single women showed the same preference. And women who described themselves as struggling financially were even *more* likely to prefer emotional security!

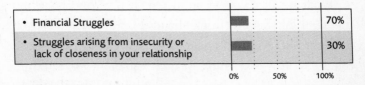

If you had to choose between these two bad choices, would you rather endure: [Choose One Answer]
Among married women:

• Financial Struggles	70%
• Struggles arising from insecurity or lack of closeness in your relationship	30%

0%   50%   100%

Security

The problem here is that what seems blazingly obvious to women is barely visible for most men—or men simply don't believe it. A few months back, a male pastor was interviewing

Shaunti onstage in front of a large group of twenty-something singles. At one point, Shaunti decided to test our emerging hypothesis on this issue, turned to the women in the audience, and asked our survey question: "If you had to choose, would you rather endure financial struggles, or would you rather endure struggles arising from insecurity or a lack of closeness in your relationship?"

Nearly every female hand went up for the "I'd rather endure financial struggles" option.

Shaunti used that demonstration as a launching point and began outlining for the women how *men* think about providing. But after a few moments, the moderator interrupted.

"I'm so sorry, Shaunti," he said, clearly flustered. "Could we back up a bit? I'm still so…shocked by what I just witnessed that I'm not hearing a word you're saying!" Much to the women's astonishment, men around the arena were nodding in agreement.

Women, you see, have an incredibly hard time believing that *we* think that *they* think financial security would ever be so important. As one woman asked in a focus group, "How could any man ever think we'd choose money over him?" Another said: "So in essence you guys are thinking that we are materialistic—really, *really* materialistic—and that we'd choose *things* over your happiness?!"

Uh…yeah. I guess that is what we're saying. But apparently, we're wrong. And for once, being wrong is very good news. Not only does the woman in your life care far more about you than anything you could provide, she's willing to sacrifice financially to have more *of* you and more happiness *for* you.

The Inner Life of Mr. Provider

Are you still skeptical? One reason this is so hard for us to accept may have nothing to do with a woman's wiring, but with ours. Shaunti's research among men for *For Women Only* demonstrated that three quarters of all men are "always" or "often" conscious of their burden to provide—*and most of us wouldn't have it any other way.*

Guys can't just demote work to some corner of our life. What we do defines us. Most days, it *is* us. That means our sense of self-worth—and a lot of other feelings—is all wrapped up in it. For example, working toward our family's financial security is an important way we show our love. It's not a big jump to then think, "Longer hours = more love." And we assume the woman we love knows it!

The problem, I found, is that she *doesn't* know it.

In fact, since what she wants is your time and attention (which creates emotional security), if you appear to give

Security

more time and attention to work, it appears that you are making work your priority. To her, that means that she is *not* your priority. That choice leaves her feeling distanced and unloved by you. Even if the main reason you're busting your tail is to show her your love.

Thankfully, there's a solution to this dilemma. To begin with, if security doesn't really mean what we thought it did, let's more closely redefine what security *does* mean to our wives.

> Let's define what "emotional security" means to our wives.

What Security Means to Her

Since most guys would never even think to put "emotional" and "security" together in the same sentence, what does such a foreign concept look like in practical terms? Here's what we learned:

1) She feels that the two of you are close;
2) She sees that you make time together a priority;
3) She sees your commitment to her;
4) She sees that you are active in the life of the home; and even,

5) She sees you making an effort to provide (as long as that doesn't crowd out 1–4).

Let's briefly outline each.

1. She feels secure when you two feel close.

Creating a sense of closeness between the two of you is more important than anything else—to a woman, it is almost a synonym for emotional security. And I was encouraged to see that it was *so easy*.

For us guys, money in the bank helps us feel safe and successful. But for women, the currency that counts is more likely to be a strong sense of closeness or intimacy with their man. In other words, your wife wants to be your love *and* your best friend…to know that she is yours and you are hers.

> For women, the currency that counts is a strong sense of closeness or intimacy with their man.

And here's the surprise for us guys: Living in the same house and even having sex doesn't necessarily mean that she feels close to you. Most married guys I know just assume a level of closeness. We share a house and a bed…how could we *not* be close?

Security

But for our wives, proximity and sex do not equal closeness. Consider the following exchange from one focus group when we asked how women felt when men traveled away from home:

> Q: Is the only cure for loneliness for him to be there?
> A: Not necessarily. And anyway, it's very easy to be lonely when he is physically there.

So what builds closeness?

So what *does* create a sense of closeness? Much of it is the little things that come along with being each other's 1) love and 2) best friend.

1) It means that she feels you belong to and love each other. Even small little gestures convey love and build closeness in a way I never would have thought. And they are so doable. Shaunti puts it this way:

> It's not that the little things somehow make a difference. It's that the little things *are* the difference between feeling secure and loved, or not. The big things—some

big romantic dinner for example—don't do that as much. They are wonderful, once in a while. But they don't come close to building the same feeling of being loved that comes from when you reach for my hand in a parking lot, or leave me a silly voice mail calling me a special nickname that's just between us.

And here's the thing, guys: I didn't *used* to do those things that much. But once I discovered that the little things were that important—well, heck: *Those* I can do!

Every woman will be touched by different little things. But let me give you an example that proves this is not rocket science. In one focus group, we were talking about what makes women feel loved, when to my surprise Shaunti began describing a recent incident. She and I had been walking through a parking lot, and I put my hand on the small of her back to steer her through some rows of cars.

Hearing that, every other woman in the room put her hand to her heart or clasped her hands together, and sighed. "Awwwww…" "Oh, that's so sweet." "What a good guy." The other man in the room and

Security

I looked at each other in utter shock. Especially since at the time I'd been worried that Shaunti might get mad at me for "telling her what to do"—since that would have been my reaction in a similar situation!

> "The little things *are* the difference between feeling secure and loved, or not."

2) *It means that she feels you two are best friends.* Being close doesn't mean that you are her best *girl* friend—expected to talk for hours—but it *does* mean that you two know each other better than anyone else.

As one woman put it: "My sense of security with my husband doesn't just come from expressing my emotions, but from knowing his." Another said, "I don't think he understands how desperately I want to be known. He's a wonderful husband, godly, attentive, but I really want him to be more interested in who I really am."

2. She feels secure when you make time together a priority.

As you might imagine, another thing that makes her feel secure is knowing that after God, she's your priority. Knowing that she and the kids come before your job and that *you care for her first* even if you feel your job is what you do to care for your family. One representative wife put it like this: "We can have plenty of money stored away and be very secure financially, but if I'm not secure about whether I'm a priority for my husband, all that money doesn't mean much. But on the other hand, if I know that he is there for me, I can face any struggles financially."

> "If I know that he is there for me, I can face any struggles financially."

For us nuance-challenged men, here's a simplified summary of what "being a priority" usually means to her: It is the amount of time and attention you give her outside of traditional work hours (meaning, outside forty or fifty hours a week) compared to anything else. Since there are only a limited number of possible "together" hours in a day, she views every above-the-norm hour spent on your work or outside interests as coming directly from the few hours she expected to spend with you.

A wife does *not* expect her husband to spend every off-the-job hour with her. But to feel emotionally secure, she can't feel that he's consistently choosing other time priorities over her. As one woman said:

Security

My husband is a very good provider, dearly loves his family, and says I complete him in every way. But he rarely seems willing to spend one-on-one time with me or to share my life, yet he always has time for the guys. I know he also needs his friends, but this lack of *me* in his day-to-day life is causing a big drift in our marriage.

3. She feels secure when you demonstrate your commitment.

Your wife needs to feel in the core of her being that nothing will scare you away and that you will do whatever you need to do to ensure that nothing comes between the two of you.

One woman put it perfectly: "I need to know that he will be there for me, no matter what. We have a good relationship, but I still need to *know* that he's not going anywhere—physically or emotionally."

One simple way to demonstrate this commitment is to use the examples of reassurance after conflict that we talked about in chapter 2.

4. She feels secure when you are active in parenting and the life of the home.

Women feel secure when they see their husband choosing to be an active participant in the life of the home, even if it means reworking other priorities. Unfortunately, if a man isn't careful, his laudable drive to provide may prevent him from taking that active role in the life the couple set out to enjoy together. Some wives felt like they started out as a general partner with their husbands, but somewhere along the way wound up as a sole proprietor.

One wife said:

> While we're not wealthy, we have some good funds saved up. But my husband seems to feel like we're always on the verge of a problem, so he has to always get that extra client, that extra paycheck, even if it means being locked in his home office all night after dinner, with no time to play with the kids. Will he ever feel that we have "enough"? I appreciate having that cushion—but not when it hurts *us*.

Another, by contrast, explained why she felt so secure:

> My husband is working hard, but I'm so grateful that he also recognizes that kids need a dad's presence as much as they need a mom's. So many of my friends are frustrated that they have to ask their husband to "babysit," as if the kids aren't his kids, too. My

husband is so wonderful about recognizing that yes, he's tired, but so am I. And the fact that he'll play with the kids or manage the dishes really gives me the sense that we're all in this together.

Further, quite a few busy moms told us that simply being appreciated by their husbands also helped them feel very secure. Any hard-working guy can understand the security that comes from feeling appreciated.

> Any hard-working guy can understand the security that comes from feeling appreciated.

5. She feels secure when you do make an effort to provide.

Lastly, after all this discussion of finances not being her top priority, you should know that the effort you make to provide for your family does add to a sense of emotional security— *even if* the results aren't bringing in the *amount* of money you assumed she wanted. Where guys focus on the results, our wife focuses on the effort—and the effort does make her feel loved as long as it doesn't crowd out the other elements of emotional security.

The women we talked to agreed that in the choice between financial insecurity and emotional insecurity, it's not that they would *enjoy* financial struggles. But they would prefer to *endure* them if they could get more of you. As one woman said, "Financial struggles, by definition, are difficult. But if I had to, I'd rather have them, than lose him."

> "Financial struggles, by definition, are difficult. But if I had to, I'd rather have them, than lose him."

Obviously, in all of this, we need to find a balance. You are designed to want to provide for your family, and women do appreciate that. None of us would want to use these "emotional security" findings as an excuse to quit our jobs, sit on the couch for hours, and eat Cheetos. Not that there is anything wrong with Cheetos—but all things in moderation.

They Want Us to Be Happy

One of our most encouraging findings was that even though women truly wanted their husband to have a job where he worked less in order to have more of his time, they also wanted their husband to have a job where he worked less so that *he* could enjoy life more. A great deal of a woman's stress and insecurity comes from knowing that her husband is working long hours at a job that causes *him* stress just to provide a certain level of income. If there was another option, most women would choose a lower-stress, lower-income job that he'd enjoy, even if it meant going through financial insecurity.

On our survey, we asked women to choose between two different job scenarios. As before, 70 percent of the women said they'd rather their husband take a lower-paying job that would require financial sacrifices if it allowed more family time. And even more fascinating, the number rises to 89 percent if they felt *you* wanted to make that choice (adding in those women who were "neutral")!

And encouragingly, even though women want emotional security and closeness, we could find none who would want their husband to take a "family-friendly" job that would make him unfulfilled or unhappy in his work life. They knew there was no emotional security in that "solution." As one wife put it, "Then I would just have a depressed man on my hands, and that would defeat the purpose!"

Put yourself in this scenario: Your husband/significant other has a very well-paying job that requires a lot of hours and emotional attention away from home. You enjoy a comfortable lifestyle and all the enrichment opportunities for the kids that come with it, but you and the children often do feel distant from your husband/significant other, and when you two are together there is often discord. Now suppose that your husband/significant other was offered a different job that he'd enjoy, that would allow much more time with family—but it would also mean a substantial pay cut and some lifestyle adjustments for your family. Which best describes your likely feelings in this scenario? [Choose One Answer]

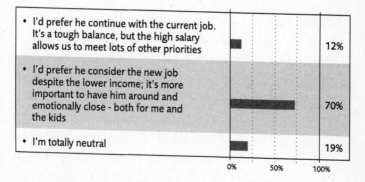

* Because of rounding, numbers slightly exceed 100%.

Rethinking Our Provider/Protector Assumptions

This whole topic boils down to asking ourselves—and asking our wives—one question: *Am I providing the type of security she genuinely wants and needs?*

One friend put his finger on the crux of the difficulty for many of us. "Men focus on income and possessions because it is so much easier to measure success in numbers. 'Loving attention' is much more difficult for us to quantify."

I started this chapter with the comment that we men often feel caught between a rock and a hard place. But we've now heard from hundreds of women that while there may be a rock on one side—her absolute need for emotional security—there is no "hard place" of absolute financial desire on the other. It's more like a "soft place," since for most women all the money and things aren't nearly the priority that *you* are. Shaunti didn't want more of me *and* the doorman building. She wanted more of me, period. And when I finally got that through my head—five years later—we moved away from New York and to a more family-friendly life in Atlanta.

And if you suspect that perhaps your wife has been trying to say the same thing...have a talk. You might be surprised at what you hear.

> For most women all the money and things aren't nearly the priority that *you* are.

What Matters: Happy Dad

We all instinctively know that as our children grow up and leave the home, as we and our wives age together, the best memories will not center around the cool things that we bought or the size of the house. Invariably, the measure of success will be something much simpler and closer to home—the life that we shared on a daily basis.

A woman who grew up in a large family in Flint, Michigan—one of those gritty, industrial cities of the Midwest—described how more "providing" by her father had not turned out to be a better life for any of them:

When we were little, we lived in a small house right in the city. The neighborhood wasn't great, but I loved my life. And my dad was a happy dad. When he was home from work, we'd all play. He was so much fun to be around.

When I was eleven, my dad wanted to provide a better future for us. And rather than just picking another house and moving out of the city, he decided to have a special home built. Since we didn't have tons of money, he knew he'd have to do a lot of the work himself. He said we were worth it.

Unfortunately, he didn't realize what all the extra stress and pressure would do—not just to him, but to us. The stress of juggling everything began to wear my dad down. We lost happy dad, and instead found grumpy dad. He stopped playing with us so much, and he was just on edge a lot, not relaxed and fun.

I now know that he was sacrificing himself to provide a better future for us kids, but we wanted *him* much more than we wanted the new house or better schools. We just wanted happy dad back.

She says that if the kids or her mom had been given the choice of the little home in Flint with happy dad or the bigger country home with grumpy dad, it would have been no contest. They all would have chosen happy dad.

"We just wanted happy dad back."

A Personal Journey Closer to Home

Every guy I know who works hard does it at least in part because he believes he's doing what is best for the family. Providing for our family is commendable and a biblical injunction. But we must be willing to ask ourselves whether we are delivering what our family genuinely needs, or whether we've somewhere bought into some internal or cultural assumptions that might actually be sabotaging what matters most. If so, some adjustments are probably in order.

I realize, looking back, that my own dad *did* make those adjustments. My dad worked long hours in the real estate business—which in the 1970s was often unstable—but when he came home and there was still some daylight left, we always threw the football around. Or he would hit fly balls to my brothers and me in the empty field beside our house. Good times.

We always had a roof over our heads and three meals a day, but I do remember feeling the stress of belt-tightening measures during times when no commissions came in. But here's the thing: Despite the pressures, and despite knowing that we didn't have some of the things that other kids had, *because of my dad's presence in our lives* I have only amazing memories of my childhood. Not a single memory centers on what we lacked, but on the things we did together.

> Because of my dad's presence in our lives, not a single memory centers on what we lacked, but on what we did *together*.

Security

Of course, cutting back financially to improve *real* quality of life does introduce its own stresses. Shaunti and I can attest to that. For the past five years, I've struggled to keep a start-up technology company alive while developing a part-time legal practice—all from a home office. Many months, we didn't know how we were going to pay the mortgage until right before it was due. Yes, that is stressful!

But we have managed, we've seen the truth that God always provides, and our family relationships are stronger than they've ever been. In fact, during one particularly tough financial season, Shaunti actually got *alarmed* when I floated the idea of going back to a big law firm! And, honestly, I wouldn't trade the time that I've been able to spend with Shaunti and the kids for any high-paying law firm job on the planet.

Chapter 5

LISTENING *IS* THE SOLUTION

Why her feeling about the problem is the problem, and how to fix your urge to fix

Listening

> *When she is sharing an emotional problem, her feelings and her desire to be heard are much more important than the problem itself.*

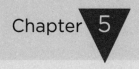

Not long ago, Shaunti and I were cleaning up after dinner when I noticed that she seemed down. She had been working long hours on several projects, so I knew she was tired. She'd also just found out that a hoped-for invitation to talk about *For Women Only* on CNN the next day had fallen through.

Supersensitive guy that I am, I probably would have stayed quiet and given her the space to work through it. But my recent work on mapping the female mind set me up to

97

try something else. *She doesn't need space*, I realized. *She needs to talk.* So I paused, dish in hand, and asked if she was okay.

> *She doesn't need space, I realized. She needs to talk.*

She sighed. "I'm just a little bummed about CNN," she said. "I know how networks work. I shouldn't have gotten my hopes up."

When I asked if she knew why it fell through, she shook her head. "Not really. They said everyone loved the topic, but when they got to the production meeting, some segments had to be cut. Nothing personal."

Since I really wanted to cheer her up, I decided the time was perfect to give Shaunti one of my best count-your-blessings pep talks. "But wow, think about what an amazing opportunity it is to even be in a position to be *considered* by CNN," I said.

"I know, but—"

"And think about what a blessing it is to be on *other* radio and TV all the time, to be able to share this message and save marriages."

"Yeah, but it's not the same as CNN."

"Oh, I don't know. You had five million viewers on that

Hollywood talk show last month." I smiled. "That's a lot of people."

To my surprise, my reasonable, well-adjusted wife suddenly got angry. "I'm trying to tell you something, and you're acting like you don't even care!" She stood up from the table and seemed to be fighting back tears.

"Huh?" She'd really caught me off guard.

My mind started whirring. *You gotta be kidding me!* I thought. *You think I don't care? What do you think I've been trying to show you? That's the last time I try to encourage you!* But, of course, I didn't say any of that. Instead I muttered two tried-and-true gems: "Okay, fine." Then I shut down and went to see what was on TV.

Does this little scenario strike you as familiar? Here's the sequence again:

1. She seems to need a listening ear.
2. You care, so you say "What's up?"
3. She reveals what's bugging her.
4. You care, so you try to help.
5. She reacts with, "Obviously, you don't care!"

Later, Shaunti and I both apologized. And later still, we were able to identify the problem in our scenario: *Apparently, what I thought was listening and caring, wasn't.* Of course, I *was* listening—using my ears, my brains, my stunningly good intentions. Really. Trouble is, it just wasn't happening in the way that *felt* like listening and caring to my wife.

> Apparently, what I thought was listening and caring, wasn't.

Now that I've seen the massive response to this issue from women around the country, I believe that learning to listen in the way women need is a huge missing-in-action skill for most guys. If you're at all like me, the issue is complicated by more bad news—you already think you listen well. Heck, you think you're a listening machine, a real superman of sympathy! Most men do. I did.

Chances are, though, we're not.

But there's good news. Men might be broke down on this issue, but we're also just a few steps away from listening habits *that actually work*. Which is what this chapter will show you.

Whether it's with your girlfriend or your wife, listening to her so she actually *feels* listened to will pay immediate dividends in a deeper, stronger, more rewarding relationship. Why? Because smart listening tells a woman louder than almost anything else that she is known, cared for, and loved. It's probably not too far off to state that smart listening has more power in her life and heart than—get this—all the things guys do first and best. Like analyzing, rescuing, deciding, doing, helping—or fixing the problem.

> Listening to her so she actually *feels* listened to will pay immediate dividends in a stronger, more rewarding relationship.

"She doesn't want you to fix it."

We've all heard, "She doesn't want you to fix it, she just wants you to listen." But even though that phrase is accurate (according to all our interviews), most guys have no idea what it means or how to do it.

I'll explain *how* in a minute, but first, here's what it means. Three things:

- *She doesn't want you to fix it* = she doesn't actually want or need your solution to the problem, at least at the beginning.
- *She just wants you to listen* = she does want and need you to understand how she's *feeling* about the problem.
- *"It"* = an emotional problem. This listening rule does not apply to technical conundrums.

Let's take these one at a time.

Listening

"She doesn't want you to fix it" = she doesn't need you to fix it.

In case you're wondering, this doesn't mean "She doesn't need you to do nothing." More on that later. Instead, the key is to understand *why* she's sharing something. And it's not—as we think—because she needs our help. In fact, our women usually feel quite capable of solving problems without any help from manly men like us. That's not what they are looking for—at least at first. Look at the results from the survey.

Even if a man provided a very "reasonable" solution to the problem under discussion, just 5 percent of women said that would actually solve their problem. Add it up, guys. 95 percent of women feel that *a reasonable solution would <u>not</u> solve their problem.*

What's more, fully 60 percent of the women felt the offered solution—no matter how reasonable—was a negative. Some appreciated their man's suggestion, some didn't, but the majority felt that it detracted from the sense that he was listening and being supportive.

To see why that is, we turn to the second and most important principle.

Suppose you had a fairly serious conflict with someone important to you, and have been dealing with strong emotions about it all day. That evening, you start to tell your husband/significant other what happened and how you feel about it. After listening for a little bit, he jumps in with a reasonable suggestion for fixing the problem. How is this most likely to make you feel? [Choose One Answer]

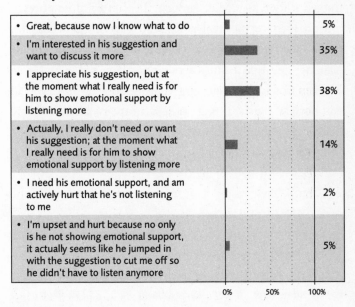

• Great, because now I know what to do	5%
• I'm interested in his suggestion and want to discuss it more	35%
• I appreciate his suggestion, but at the moment what I really need is for him to show emotional support by listening more	38%
• Actually, I really don't need or want his suggestion; at the moment what I really need is for him to show emotional support by listening more	14%
• I need his emotional support, and am actively hurt that he's not listening to me	2%
• I'm upset and hurt because no only is he not showing emotional support, it actually seems like he jumped in with the suggestion to cut me off so he didn't have to listen anymore	5%

0%   50%   100%

Listening

*Because of rounding, answers do not exactly total 100%.

"She just wants you to listen" = she wants you to focus on her feelings, not the problem.

She's not sharing something so you can fix it; she's sharing it so you can understand how she *feels* about something that is bothering her.

Here's the thing: For most of our lives, we men have trained ourselves to cut through the clutter of emotion in order to focus on the "real issue." Instead, we need to grasp the single most important key to being a good listener: For our wife, her negative feelings about a problem *are* the real issue. In other words, the *feelings* are what she is trying most to share and have understood, even more than the problem itself.

> We have trained ourselves to cut through the clutter of emotion in order to focus on the "real issue." But for her, those feelings *are* the real issue.

Her need to get her feelings heard explains something that has confused many of us: *If she doesn't want me to fix it,* we wonder, *why does she keep talking about it?* Look at these revealing comments from women:

- "Most men feel they have to fix areas of concern for the wife and family. But when he jumps in before I am finished, he proves he isn't interested in listening to something that is important to me. This leaves me feeling devalued."

- "A few days ago, I was telling my husband about a long-standing relationship tension I have with someone. It was so sweet that he just listened, showed me his concern and said, 'I don't know if it's going to get better, honey.' I felt so heard."
- "Just being able to share what's going on *actually fixes* something for a woman!"

"Just being able to share what's going on *actually fixes* something for a woman!"

Listening

"It" = an emotional problem, not a technical one.

The "she doesn't want you to fix it" mantra has confused many of us because we know some situations require a fix. So here's how you know the difference: If it's an area of emotional concern, apply listening skills. If it's not, apply fixing skills.

Apply listening skills to areas that define a woman's relationships, well-being, and sense of self-worth. Home stresses, for example. Work. Friendships. Conflicts.

You.

This simply doesn't apply to those times when your wife

tells you something is starting to howl under the gear shift in her Toyota and what should we do? In such cases, you can safely put away your gender translation gear. You can even forget her feelings—as in, "Honey, how does that make you feel when the transmission does that?" Just go male and fix away to your heart's content—as in, "I'll take it in to the shop tomorrow."

For any man who wants to be a good listener, the good news is that we don't have to shut off our "Mr. Fix-it" nature. We just have to apply those skills to the right problem. This kind of response may feel more like *not* responding at first. More like failure or weakness or not caring. But it's genius— and even relationship klutzes can figure it out.

Just like we did running the bases back in school.

> We just have to apply those fix-it skills to the right problem.

How to Listen (Think Baseball)

It's true; when life gets confusing, I turn to baseball. The elegance of the game. The history. The lazy afternoons in the outfield bleachers. The '84 Tigers. (Yeah, it's been a tough couple of decades for me.)

You know I'm right. Baseball explains almost everything.

So okay, here's my guide to running the listening bases. I doubt base running is how marriage counselors define good listening, but it works, it's supported by the evidence, and it's a plan I can remember.

- **First Base:** Give her your full physical attention.
- **Second Base:** Give her your full mental attention.
- **Third Base:** Listen for the right thing—how she *feels* about the problem.
- **Home Plate:** Acknowledge and affirm her feelings about the problem.

Now you probably think you already know *and* do all these things. But let's take the bases one by one, adding what most men *think* they mean.

Rounding First

Give her your full physical attention.
(What most men think: "I can listen well even if I'm doing something else.")

Seems like men easily confuse listening with hearing. Our definition of listening might be something like: "She's talking, and I'm hearing what she's saying, therefore I'm listening."

Even if I'm watching *American Chopper* at the same time.

But that's treating a person like a signal source. And if you think about it, that's what inattention tells the other person—"You're making noise, and you're one among several data inputs I'm processing at this moment."

To move from simply hearing to genuinely receiving what another person is saying, we have to take our attention *off* every other distraction and put it *on* her. More than likely, that means facing her, looking at her, staying in the same room as her. It may also mean running interference when other distractions threaten.

For example, a year later, Shaunti can still remember a simple physical gesture I did when she really needed to talk and the kids kept interrupting. I asked the kids to play elsewhere for a minute, pulled her into the living room, sat down with her on the sofa, and asked her to share what was on her mind. Those two or three minutes were an incredibly good investment if they still make her feel loved a year later! And I have to confess: I have absolutely no memory of this event. Not because I do this all the time, but rather because it took so little time or effort!

If physical listening just doesn't seem possible, I've found it's better to fess up to the challenge. Ask for a rain check.

Suggest, "Could we talk about this later when we can be alone (when I'm not so tired)? I want to be able to really hear you, and honestly, I can't now."

▲ Those two or three minutes were an incredibly good investment if they still make her feel loved a year later!

Rounding Second

Give her your full mental attention.
(What most men think: "If I'm listening, I'm not doing anything.")

When Shaunti and I were living in New York City, one of our friends was an acoustic engineer who designed opera houses. He seemed like the perfect candidate for the old question, "If a tree falls in a forest and no one is there to hear it, does it make a sound?"

He answered quite seriously. "No, it doesn't. It makes a *noise*, but sound has to be perceived. The sound waves have to be listened to in order for the noise to be a sound. Just them hitting a tree stump or a rock doesn't count."

We can apply the same idea to listening. If we're just sitting there, not actually paying attention to what our wife is saying, we might as well be a stump. Listening isn't "I'll sit here and let her bombard me." It is an active practice of identifying her feelings, considering what's she's really saying, and listening for the story behind the story.

That's why listening isn't the same thing as "doing nothing." And that's why real listening can really wear a guy out. Because most women don't have an emotional and even physical limit on their ability to listen and process emotion, they don't understand that most men do. They don't realize it is almost a physical limitation, like the mental equivalent of cardiovascular capacity.

I can be totally willing to listen to Shaunti share her feelings about something. But just like my body would shut down if I tried to run too many miles, my brain just starts checking out after a while, whether or not I want it to.

The key is to set yourself up for success by mentioning this to your wife or girlfriend at some neutral time. Use this book, point to this section, and explain the limits of your particular listening capacity. Then, when you *are* in an emotionally charged conversation for a little too long and you start to zone out, you can tell her, "I'm so sorry, I totally missed that. I'm reaching the end of my ability to hear." Blame it on you—not her.

Finally, realize that "listening" doesn't usually mean a marathon. As one male marriage counselor told us, "Guys need to know that their wives aren't looking to them to be their best girlfriend and listen for hours. For most women, even taking a fifteen-minute walk with them a few evenings a week would totally fill their need."

"Listening" doesn't usually mean a marathon.

Rounding Third

**Listen for the right thing—
how she *feels* about the problem.
(*What most men think: "I should filter out all
that emotion and listen for the facts."*)**

If you want to make it home, you have to round third base. As we said earlier, when men are faced with a problem with emotional dimensions, we turn task oriented. Put emotions in one box, objective circumstances in another, then ignore the emotion box in order to nail a solution.

But this sets us up for big trouble. We're busy trying to filter *out* a wife's feelings because we think they get in the way of solving the real problem—instead of holding the key to the real problem. We think that she's getting "too emotional" and it is clouding her thinking—never realizing that for most women, not only are their feelings the main point, but they're probably also perfectly capable of analytical thought *and* strong emotions at the same time. They just need to have their feelings listened to in order to "get somewhere."

So in order to listen *in the way she needs*, we have to do what does not come naturally and—at least at first—not present a solution. We have to retrain ourselves to do something that will initially seem even weirder. Instead of filtering out her feelings to concentrate on the problem, we need to practice filtering out the problem so we can concentrate on her feelings about it.

> We need to practice filtering out the problem so we can concentrate on her feelings about it.

In the CNN example, Shaunti didn't need a pep talk, and she didn't need my stellar business advice about how to approach CNN in a new way. All those things had already occurred to her. What she needed was a hug, and for me to hear and acknowledge her feelings. As in, "I'm so sorry—I know you were excited about being on CNN and you must be really disappointed."

If you are ever confused about what the situation requires, women suggested that a guy just ask. "Sweetheart, do you want my help, or do you just want me to listen?" (And then remember that what you need to listen to are her feelings.)

Safe at Home

Acknowledge and affirm her feelings about the problem. (What most men think: "If she could just learn not to let her feelings control her, she'd be happier.")

Now you know: She deeply needs to know that you understand how she's feeling. But put yourself in her shoes: She has absolutely no idea if you do understand unless you *show* it. Acknowledging to her what you're hearing—a simple verbal restatement of her words—is the magic bullet.

Thus, when I say to Shaunti, "That must have been so disappointing that CNN didn't come through," my circle is complete. I've run the bases and *solved her real problem.*

Shaunti tells me there are actually two types of acknowledgement, and both are important.

1. *Acknowledge what her feeling is:* "You felt disappointed."

But there's more, and this is where guys tend to trip.

2. *Affirm and sympathize with her feelings, even if you disagree with her thoughts.*

If acknowledging her feelings comes out as, "I'm sorry you felt disappointed," then affirming them means saying, "And it's okay that you felt disappointed." If you think about it, there's no such thing as a "right" or "wrong" feeling. We may disagree with the accuracy of an *assumption* that leads to that feeling, but if she's feeling something, she's feeling it. And it's not helpful or even respectful to try to talk her out of it.

> Affirming her feelings means saying, "It's okay that you felt disappointed."

Here's what several female respondents told us on this point:

- "Trying to talk me out of my feelings doesn't accomplish what he's trying to accomplish. In fact, it makes me feel absolutely terrible, like my husband doesn't care one jot about how I feel."
- "Men don't realize the value of affirming our feelings when they seem irrational or out of proportion to them. If a man could just grasp the value of that, he could cut arguments or long discussion times in half."

Now, of course there may be a need at some point to talk things through if you do disagree. But during a time of emotional sharing, it's totally counterproductive to say (even if we believe it), "You shouldn't feel that way."

WARNING: DON'T TRY THESE AT HOME!
"How *not* to listen."

There's nothing more dismaying to a guy than when he's sincerely trying to win (to be loving and helpful), but he only commits an error. She gets hurt or angry or both. Suddenly, the man is the problem. Some collected coaching advice: In the heat of an inning, *never*...

- tell her she's overreacting,
- question her version of the facts,
- wonder aloud about the time of the month,
- ask her to quit crying, or
- offer spiritual correction ("Are you sure you're not just envious?")

Listening

Getting Personal

I'll be the first to admit that when emotions start flying around, especially if the conversation is about our relationship, I can quickly conclude that my wife is attacking *me*. If Shaunti feels unhappy, I—like most men—I assume that she thinks that I blew it.

But I'm realizing that, usually, a man's performance isn't even on his wife's mind. Instead, since most women process thoughts and feelings by talking about them, they need to be able to get their feelings about the relationship out on the table and have us listen. And the only way they can do that is if we don't get defensive and take it personally.

Consider what one survey taker said she most wished her husband knew:

> That when I tell him how I feel inside about something concerning our relationship, that I am just trying to share my feeling with him so we can discuss it. He takes it as criticism and turns it around so I feel like the bad guy for bringing it up. He says, "I never do anything right," or "I can never please you," which isn't true. And so the problem never really gets discussed. I wish he could understand that it's important for me to be able to talk about these things and understand that I'm not just being critical.

When things get personal, we need to resist the natural male instinct to run for cover, man the defenses, or—worst of all—reach for the big guns. Much better to set aside our natural defensiveness and focus on listening well *even though we feel under attack*. Because we're probably not. Instead, it's usually an important opportunity to invest in our relationship and show her love in a way she will really *feel* it.

> It's an opportunity to invest in our relationship and show her love in a way she will really *feel* it.

Listening

Realize: She *Does* Appreciate You

If we get the listening sequence right, the right and healing solutions will follow. We've already seen that 60 percent of the women on the survey found suggestions to be a negative if their husbands weren't listening first, and being emotionally supportive. But next we asked, when the women set aside how they felt about their man's emotional support, how would they feel about his actual suggestions? The response was overwhelming. More than two-thirds said they were "helpful" suggestions—and we can infer that more than 80 percent actually *agreed* with the suggested solution! Just 19 percent said that the solution itself would not be a good one.

Consider times when you have actually been in the type of situation described in the previous question. Setting aside how you feel about your husband/significant other's emotional support, how useful or valuable are his actual suggestions? [Choose One Answer]

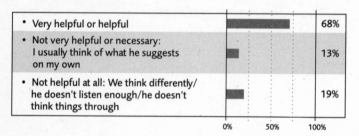

• Very helpful or helpful		68%
• Not very helpful or necessary: I usually think of what he suggests on my own		13%
• Not helpful at all: We think differently/ he doesn't listen enough/he doesn't think things through		19%

0%   50%   100%

Virtually all the data in this chapter point to one often-overlooked principle for a man who wants a happy relationship: *The person who listens well holds enormous power.*

If we can learn to listen the way she needs us to, we have great power to defuse conflicting emotions, power to acknowledge and affirm—and yes, power to *then* help find solutions.

Most of all though, when you and I listen, we wield great power to tell the woman we care about most that she is truly loved. As one woman told us, "After a great conversation I just want to kiss him and tell him how very, very much I appreciate him."

Chapter 6

WITH SEX, HER "NO" DOESN'T MEAN YOU

How her desires are impacted by her unique wiring, and why your ego shouldn't be

Physically, women tend to crave sex less often than men do—and it is usually <u>not</u> related to your desirability.

Sex

This chapter will be the ultimate test of your manhood. I'm going to ask you to do two things, and do them at the same time:

1. Think clearly
2. About sex

I've noticed, and probably so have you, that what us men do so well as separate tasks—clear thinking and sex—we routinely, embarrassingly, miserably fail at doing together.

As I found out after I got a full dose of the honest truth from about 450 women in Colorado. There I was, the only guy, listening while Shaunti presented what she'd learned about men while writing *For Women Only*. It was a weird and wonderful experience.

And here was the wonderful part—at least at first. During a lively question and answer session, almost *all* the questions focused on sex! I was so amazed at the ladies' one-track minds, I could barely listen to the questions. Back home in Atlanta, my buddies and I were ecstatic at the idea that women really *did* want sex more than we'd thought.

Fast forward to Jeff and Shaunti doing in-depth focus groups of women for this book. I am over the weirdness by now, but unfortunately, the wonderful is no longer in sight. Instead, what I'm hearing doesn't jibe *at all* with the good news I'd heard in the Rockies. Finally, I do my best to describe for these women the absolute obsession with sex among their counterparts at higher elevations.

The women stare at me politely. Then one breaks the news. "Well, um, since Shaunti's book emphasized how central sex is to a man's emotional well-being, the women were probably wondering how to handle their man's requests."

Okay, I think to myself. *Cool. Nothing wrong with that!*

She sees that clear thinking has yet to occur. "And it was

not because they want sex so much," she continues. "A lot of women don't have that same need to *pursue* sex as much as guys do. So they were simply trying to figure out what on earth to do!"

In desperation, I shoot a questioning look at my wife. But Shaunti is already nodding. "I'm afraid so," she says. "That's exactly what was happening."

The Big, Whopping Miss

How could I—a smart, married, and extremely likable man—have completely missed a full dose of the honest truth about sex from 450 women? And I hadn't just missed it. What I had *thought* I heard was almost the *direct opposite* of what they were actually saying.

After spending hours going over surveys and listening to focus groups, I've come to believe that my big, whopping miss is pretty much what men do in marriages every day. We think male and female humans are the same creatures, only with different and nicely matching body parts. We assume we have the same sexual wiring. So when there seems to be a mismatch, we have no idea why. As one of my puzzled buddies put it, "If sex is free and it's fun, why does she not want *lots* of free fun?"

▲ "If sex is free and it's fun, why does she not want lots of free fun?"

Now, we do know that in some marriages it's the woman who is pining for more—one in four, according to our survey. So if you are in that situation, you are not alone. And of course some wives indicated that they and their husbands were happily on the same page—to the envy of all. But since we have limited space, we're focusing just on the apparent majority of husbands that want "more and better," and don't know what to do about it.*

Thankfully, solutions exist, and our research confirms good news for men who find themselves in that situation. In particular: Most women do care about what their man wants. And they *do* care about sex. And they *do* want great sexual relationships with their husband.

But to get there, we need to do that "thinking clearly" thing.

The Impossible Surprise About Sex with Her: "It's not you..."

If you're a typical married male, you probably want more sex with your wife than you get. But that's not the end of the

---

* That said, if you do find yourself in the 25% of marriages where your wife is the one wanting more, and would like a resource that includes discussion of that situation, we recommend the book *A Celebration of Sex* by Dr. Douglas E. Rosenau.

story. I know, because in Shaunti's professional survey for *For Women Only*, 97 percent of men said "getting enough sex" wasn't, by itself, enough—they wanted to feel genuinely wanted.

Men are powerfully driven by the emotional need to feel *desired* by our wives, and we filter everything through that grid: *Do I feel desired or not desired by my wife?* If we feel our wife truly wants us sexually, we feel confident, powerful, alive, and loved. If we don't, we feel depressed, angry, and alone. And this goes way beyond the amount of sex we're having.

But here's where the first breakdown in communication comes between the average husband and wife. Our surveys showed a startling, hard-to-believe, but oddly encouraging truth for men:

While you want to be genuinely desired by your wife, her lower level of desire for sex likely has nothing to do with your desirability.

You might want to read that again. And if you think about it, that's actually good news for the 99.9 percent of us who don't look like Tom Cruise.

Here are the facts: Among survey takers who wanted less sex than their husbands, fully 75 percent indicated that it had *nothing* to do with his desirability, sexual prowess, or general studliness. In fact, of the remaining 25 percent, less than *4 percent* said their lower interest in sex was specifically because their husband was "not attractive or desirable"! (The hesitation of the other 21 percent primarily had to do with not anticipating pleasure, including for physical reasons.)

> ▽ While you want to be genuinely desired by your wife, her lower level of desire for sex likely has nothing to do with your desirability.

One survey taker spoke for that whopping 96 percent of women when she said that the one thing she most wished her husband knew was "that just because I do not want sex as often as he does, I still love him deeply and find him very attractive."

Look on the next page at the top three reasons (by a wide margin) that women gave for wanting less sex.

Our results show that although there certainly are factors that can be addressed, the frequency gap is usually *not* because a wife doesn't desire her husband. In the great majority of cases, the cliché is actually true: "Look, it's not you. It's me."

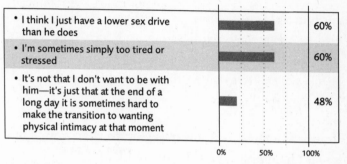

Answered by women who said they wanted less sex than their husbands.*

• I think I just have a lower sex drive than he does	60%
• I'm sometimes simply too tired or stressed	60%
• It's not that I don't want to be with him—it's just that at the end of a long day it is sometimes hard to make the transition to wanting physical intimacy at that moment	48%

0%   50%   100%

* Because women could choose more than one answer, percentages did not add up to 100%.

⬡ The frequency gap is usually *not* because a wife doesn't desire her husband.

Sex

If you're still thinking clearly, your brain has ground to a halt on an apparent impossibility: *But I can't imagine finding my wife very attractive, being in love with her, and <u>not</u> wanting to have sex with her often! So how could she be that way?*

But remember, that's guy thinking, and we're trying to learn *her* thinking. For the moment, take a step away from that seeming impossibility, and let your driving question instead be:

"So if it's not about me, what *is* it about?

"So if it's not about me...?": Five Truths About Women and Sex

Shaunti and I want to relay what women around the country told us about their sexual wiring, and what they want to give—and get—from their man. These five revelations, should you choose to believe them, have the potential to radically improve this area of your marriage.

Truth #1. She has a lower sex drive than you—and she'd change that fact if she could.

Physiological fact #1: Experts explain that the average woman simply has less testosterone and other sexually assertive hormones than the average man, and therefore has less of an urge to *pursue* sex. This doesn't mean she doesn't want it, or won't enjoy it once it's happening, but just that seeking it out isn't usually on her mind.

> This doesn't mean she doesn't want it, or won't enjoy it once it's happening, but seeking it out isn't usually on her mind.

Most men know this fact, but—physiological fact #2—we forget it on a regular basis. Like every evening. We forget because we can't really feel the truth of it, especially when she says or implies "no" the minute we show sexual interest. Admit it—analysis of physiological differences is not where your mind goes following another nonencounter.

So let's step back and look at some implications of her physiology:

▶ *Lower level of sexually assertive hormones = less craving for sex*

Not *no* craving, mind you, just *less*. It's a fact, and we need to stop assuming it has something to do with *us*.

As several experts explained, this is a complex issue, but it boils down to the fact that there are actually two different types of desire. Where men have more testosterone-type hormones linked to "assertive" sexual desire, women have more estrogen, which is tied to what is called "receptive" sexual desire. Which means that they tend to be *available*, but simply don't have as much craving to pursue it.* And recent studies have shown that a common form of birth control (the Pill) can reduce libido even further.

It doesn't help that movies, television shows, and advertisements seem to imply that all women would be sexually charged bimbo wannabes if you were just enough of a stud.

On the survey, when we asked women what they most

Sex

---

* The book *A Celebration of Sex* by Dr. Douglas E. Rosenau addresses the physiological issues in more detail.

wished their husbands understood, one wife put it this way, "I want him to know I don't love him less just because my sex drive isn't as strong as his."

▶ *Lower level of sexually assertive hormones = less likely to initiate sex*

As one book put it, "Receptive doesn't necessarily mean passive [but] available, and perhaps willing, but without the initiative...."* Related to this, we received a fascinating e-mail not long ago from a man whose wife had read Shaunti's book, *For Women Only*.

> My wife then explained to me that she simply has no physical drive to pursue sex. When we are having sex, she says that she loves it. The problem is that otherwise, sex just never occurs to her whereas there is never a time when it does *not* occur to me! Thankfully, after reading *For Women Only*, my wife understood how important sex really is to me and has even begun to initiate sex. She does it because she wants to show that she loves me. It works...

* Full quote from Page 125 of *The Alchemy of Love and Lust*, by Theresa Crenshaw. "The biochemical urge we call the sex drive comes in two basic styles: aggressive and receptive. The aggressive sex drive is controlled not just by testosterone, as most people think, but by vasopressin, DHEA, serotonin, dopamine, and LHRH as well. The receptive sex drive...has been overlooked altogether.... Receptive doesn't necessarily mean passive [but] available, and perhaps willing, but without the initiative to pursue sex."

In one focus group, a woman said this:

> I just don't feel that drive to go after physical pleasure as often. For me, it's about once every ten days that *I'm* the one looking for the physical pleasure. The other times are because he needs it. And from my standpoint, it's time to be together, it's uninterrupted time, it's a way to have his undivided attention. Not that it's not physically great once we get started—it is! It's just that for me, there's usually not the drive to start.

▶ *Lower level of sexually assertive hormones = more susceptibility to nonsexual distractions*

Sex

Like a noise from the kid's room. Like a headache. Like stress or leftover thoughts from her day. Like exhaustion.

She's not making it up. In relation to her lower sex drive, she's more sensitive to hindrances, and feels them more intensely than you or I would. As one woman said, "For guys, it seems, sex provides relief or escape from exhaustion. For women, we have to pull ourselves out of exhaustion in order to want to have sex."

> ⚠ She's more sensitive to hindrances, and feels them more intensely than you or I would.

But there's reassuring news, too. Not only is the woman in your life not making up the hindrances to sex she experiences, *she would readily change her sexual responsiveness if she could.* Look at the data:

(Answered by women who said they wanted less sex than their husbands.)

If you could magically change your sex drive and/or some of the reasons you don't want sex as much as your husband does, would you? [Choose One Answer]

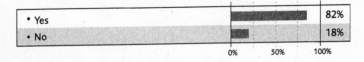

• Yes	82%
• No	18%

0%   50%   100%

You can see that more than eight out of ten wives would prefer to want sex as much as their husbands…if they could. (And among happily married women, that desire was almost 100 percent.)

Truth #2. She needs more warm-up time than you.

A guy's sexual motor is pretty much always running. Pop the clutch and go. Not so for a woman. But once her sexual motor is warmed up and running, she is fine and raring to go, just like we are.

One respondent told us:

> I wish my husband would understand that as much as I love to be intimate with him, there are times when it takes a long time to "get me there." I have been busy running after kids all day, cleaning, cooking, etc. Sex also helps me to unwind, but I need a little help. He seems to think that just because he is ready and set, I should be too. He gets frustrated because I do not seem like I am enjoying him, but if he would just take his time, we would both enjoy the experience more.

Another woman provided a great word picture.

> It's not that I don't *want* to make love, but at the end of a long day with four kids, my mind is set on a course like a cruise ship headed for port...port being that quiet bit of space a mom anticipates when the kids are asleep, the chores done, and the house quiet. And just as I'm within sight of that port, my hubby rolls over and says, "Whatcha doing over there?" It's not that I don't want to be with

Sex

him, but, mentally, it's like trying to stop a cruise ship that's going full steam ahead and making it turn on a dime. I can't quite turn off the day and do an about-face in the blink of an eye like he can.

Many other women echoed what one said she most wished her husband knew: "How much I truly and deeply love him, but my body just doesn't have the same sexual drive as his *until we are engaged in the act* [emphasis mine]. Then I'm *very* into it."

The "very into it" part is great news. But to get there, what this means in practice is one of two things. Either 1) she needs you to take it slow, to give her brain a chance to catch up, or even better, 2) she needs some "anticipation time."

> Either she needs you to take it slow, or she needs some "anticipation time."

I know us guys think that if we were desirable enough, sex would just be spontaneous because our wife couldn't keep her hands off us. But remember—her engine isn't warmed up yet. Look at the "anticipation" example one woman shared:

My husband and I don't get too many nights alone, but we carved out a dinner date one night, and while we were having dinner he whispered in my ear, "I can't wait to get home and have my dessert." I knew the dessert was me, and I don't think I've ever eaten so fast in my life. I couldn't wait to get home.

Truth #3. Your body (no matter how much of a stud you are) does not by itself turn on her body.

Maybe you should sit down. Take a breath. Clear that head. Because average male assumptions simply will *not* work here.

Let's start with how *you* work. Your eyes see an attractive woman, and generally your body registers attraction. Instantly. If the attractive woman isn't wearing much, your physical reaction is even stronger. It's like metal shavings getting pulled toward a magnet.

Your wife, though, is not like you. She is not sexually aroused simply by seeing you at your studly best. If you are looking particularly handsome or sexy, she *will* notice, and she *will* find you attractive. But—get this—*her body is still not lusting over your body.*

Listen in to an actual conversation one long-married couple relayed to us:

She, delivering the shocking news: "There isn't one thing about your body that makes me sexually attracted to you and want to go to bed with you."

He, disbelieving: "I thought I was sexy and good looking. You always told me I was!"

She, calmly: "You are. But that has nothing to do with why I want to have sex with you."

Noting his blank look, she continues: "Really. Nothing about your naked body makes me hot—that is, until *after* we're sexually involved."

He, sputtering: "But...I...how...?"

She, reassuring: "Babe, I like you, and I like your naked body. It's sweet, actually, and you're mine. But it's not like my body is lusting after yours."

He, grasping: "What...what about me in my black leather jacket? You always come up to me and growl. Are you saying...?"

She: "Nope, even you in that jacket. You look totally hot, mind you, and I do want to be with you.

But I'm just telling you, physically my body does not become sexually aroused *one bit!*"

The truth for all us average Joes is that our wives can find us desirable and attractive—but still not be turned on by that alone. Women get turned on in other, more out of sight but equally powerful ways. And that leads to another fact about sex that most guys have heard over and over...but have never quite come to terms with.

> Women get turned on in other, more out of sight but equally powerful ways.

4. For her, sex starts in her heart.

Her body's ability to respond to you sexually is tied to how she feels *emotionally* about you at the moment. If she's not feeling anything in her heart, her body's sex switches are all the way over on "Off." Even if you put on your black leather jacket.

One consequence: Where you might greatly desire her even though she was rude to you this morning, how *you* treated *her* this morning really matters. She's not keeping score, by the way. She just can't help it. For her, those two things—what's in her heart about you and how she can respond sexually—meld into one.

■ For her, what's in her heart about you and how she can respond sexually meld into one.

One woman explained it to her husband this way: "All my power to turn you on is how I look. But where *you* have power, and where I don't, is how you treated me today. It's all emotional."

We talked a lot about your wife's need for closeness and affirmation—how to "treat her today"—in chapters 2 and 4. Bet you didn't realize we were talking about sex, too!

Of course, there's a reverse consequence of her "start in the heart" need: the potential for hurt feelings. Shaunti's honest thought here is that if a relationship has become strained, and a wife says, "The only time you're interested in me is for sex," realize that by definition, she's feeling neglected—and perhaps even used.

Now, you may be initiating sex *in order* to try to "make it better" and get those feelings of closeness back, but women aren't wired that way. If they are feeling serious emotional distance or hurt, sex does not fix it—and it may exacerbate it.

Truth #5. She wants pleasure as much as you do—and if it's not happening, she may be reluctant.

Okay. This might be difficult, but face it we must: Some wives don't experience pleasure when they are intimate with their husbands. According to our survey, this is only an issue for a relatively small minority—just 16 percent said that was why they desired less sex. But that means it is still an issue in one out of every six or seven marriages. And only if we are willing to bring up this subject with our wife, set aside our defenses, and hear what she has to say, are we going to learn if this has been a reason for her lack of interest.

One woman wrote to Shaunti:

> Men think women aren't as interested in sex as they are. But some men need to know that their wives are just not experiencing sexual satisfaction. Although they might be enjoying the process, they may not be 'finishing' it. This is a difficult subject, and many women don't want to talk about it because they don't want to depress their husband or make him feel inadequate. So they protect his feelings at the expense of their own. But if a woman isn't crossing the finish line, running the race just isn't going to be as important to her—which only makes it easier to find excuses to sit it out.

I suppose you and I only have to think about what it would be like if we always "went there" sexually only to never "get there" to know how frustrating and demotivating that would be.

Sex

Clearly, it's time for you and me to sweep up our rattled egos, maybe throw on our black leather jacket just for luck, and go looking for answers.

A Guide for Ordinary Husbands

When one of my friends heard that we were writing this chapter, he chuckled. "If you can get the average husband sex even a dozen more times a year, men will build statues to you in city parks across the country."

So the following is my stab at immortality.

Think of these practical suggestions as directions on a map—directions that apply those little-understood truths we talked about and get the two of you where you both want to be.

> ▽"If you can get the average husband sex even a dozen more times a year, men will build statues to you in city parks across the country."

1) Pay attention to her—it's the little things.

Great sex starts with helping your wife feel happy and close to you outside the bedroom.

On the survey we asked each woman who wanted less or the same amount of sex what their husband could do to increase the chances that they would want to make love more frequently. Look at the top three responses:

Are there things that your husband can do to increase the chances that you will want to make love more frequently? Please rate the helpfulness of each of the following statements. [Choose One Answer For Each Statement]

	NOT PARTICULARLY HELPFUL	VERY HELPFUL
• Maintain or increase his level of emotional attention to me	27%	73%
• Create a context where he often shows me little gestures of love throughout the day	29%	71%
• Engage in caring listening and conversation regularly	33%	67%

Sex

Great sex starts with helping your wife feel happy and close to you outside the bedroom.

Throughout this book, we show that all those "helpful" things that build closeness are really the day-to-day things—like these examples from other chapters:

- Putting your hand on the small of her back to guide her through a parking lot
- Reassuring her of your love when you two are at odds
- Getting up from the dinner table to get the fire starter so she can "close the window" and enjoy dinner
- Listening for her feelings and saying, "I'm so sorry you were disappointed, honey"

2. Give chase, Agent 007. (The time for pursuit is...always.)

I love this comment that came in to Shaunti's website: "A woman needs to feel sexy to her man. But many men do not spend the time or effort in affirming their spouse sexually *outside* of the bedroom. That means when we're in the bedroom, it's difficult for the woman to figure out whether he really wants her or whether he's just trying to satisfy his own need. A woman who knows she is sexy to her husband outside the bedroom will never have an excuse at lovemaking time!"

Another married woman told us:

Women want to be romantically pursued. It's as powerful as the man's sex drive. Men think woman can't resist James Bond because of his body, his money, or his fast cars. But that stuff is almost irrelevant. James Bond is *romantic*. He pursues a woman, flirts with her, woos her. I think women are a lot more aware of the need to work hard at meeting their man's sex-drive needs than men are aware of the need to work at meeting her romantic-pursuit needs. Guys have to realize that for a woman, they go hand in hand!

"Women want to be romantically pursued. It's as powerful as the man's sex drive."

Whether it's calls, notes, conversations, or simply admiring eye contact, the whole point of pursuit to a woman is that you notice her, you're interested in her, and you belong to her...and she belongs to *you*. Remember chapter 2? There will never be a day when she permanently feels loved. She needs to feel, day to day, that you are choosing her all over again.

3. Warm her up.

Us guys need no transition time and can have sex on our minds with a moment's notice. But since most women can't, we need to think about ways to get her "anticipation engine" running several hours in advance.

One woman showed how simple that can be. "One thing that will help get a wife in the mood is something as small as a flirting call or an e-mail. Something like, 'I saw you getting dressed this morning and I can't stop thinking about you. I can't wait to see you undress tonight.'"

That's an easy chip shot if I ever saw one.

◇ That's an easy chip shot if I ever saw one.

Another woman proposed something that other women agreed might be helpful for some, as "unspontaneous" as it sounds to men:

> With kids and jobs, for me, sex needs to be planned and expected or it just won't happen. He thinks having set days to expect it means that it is just another thing to check off my to-do list. But actually, when I have it in mind to expect it, then it is really a reward at the end of a long day. If I don't know to expect it, then that *is* when it becomes a chore and just another thing that needs to get done. The planning means I am making him a priority, not putting him on a list.

4. Sometimes, hug her just to hug her.

One main reason to create day-to-day closeness—even if no sex is on the agenda that night—is that women can spot the signs that sex *is* on the agenda and assume that your sweet gestures are not sweet at all, but are just sex-motivated. At its worst, we look like we only care about our wife when we want sex.

Now, us guys know that's not true. But unfortunately it *is* true that in the busyness of life, we sometimes simply forget about doing the loving little things just because we love our wives, so the thought of sex becomes a sort of trigger to remember to be a bit more attentive.

What that means is that we have *actually* trained our wives to be cynical and suspect total self-interest on our part whenever they see those attentive gestures. So there's a need for a little reconditioning. We need to hug our wife, send her a sweet e-mail during the day, rub her back, help her out around the house, cuddle with her in bed…and not ask for sex. At least sometimes.

5. Help her around the house. It helps you.

On the survey, about 60 percent of women interviewed said that simple helpfulness around the house would increase the likelihood that they would want to make love more

Sex

frequently—if only because they would have more energy! As you'd expect, the margin was significantly higher (up to 70 percent) among women who worked outside the home or had school-age kids.

As one stay-at-home mom said, "My husband and I have a little joke between us. I say, 'Honey, there is nothing more sexy than watching you clean something. And there's *really* nothing more sexy than watching you clean the toilet!' It's all about feeling that he wants to take care of me."

This is not just anecdotal opinion, either. A recent study by famed marriage psychologist John Gottman found that men who do more housework have both happier marriages *and* better sex lives.

Picking up the broom or doing dishes after a hard day on the job isn't exactly...well, what you were thinking when you were thinking you couldn't wait to get home! But as Gottman found, this kind of sacrificial support can often be more impressive than a dozen roses.

6. Don't take "not tonight" personally— use it as a learning tool.

As we've seen, in almost every instance, she doesn't *mean* it personally, it is not the "rejection" that you think it is, and it says literally nothing about her desire for you. Yes, it *feels* like rejection and it feels personal. But if we can think clearly on this one, we can actually bring more fulfillment to both parties.

Next time, try this: Use her "not tonight, dear" as a learning tool to understand *why* she's saying no. I'll bet your eyes will be opened to new ways to love and support your wife that perhaps you hadn't noticed before. You can get off the merry-go-round of feeling helplessly deprived and actually *do something about it.*

> You can get off the merry-go-round of feeling helplessly deprived and actually *do something about it.*

7. Clean up your act.

Several women, upon finding out that we were writing this chapter, asked Shaunti privately, "You will tell them to brush their teeth, won't you?" Quite a few women told us that the most basic hygiene would make the difference between wanting to be intimate, or not. Back when we were dating, we never would have forgotten to brush our teeth or take a shower before a date—so why do that to our wife now?

As one woman put it, "I want him just to brush his teeth regularly. And I'd like him to shave his face whiskers before we do the wild thing!"

Sex

8. When in doubt, ask her.

Just like the existence of this whole chapter, this particular "to do" runs against the grain of my middle-class, Midwestern, don't-talk-about-sex reticence. While it may not be comfortable, you just need to ask your wife what she likes, what she doesn't, and how to improve. And make sure she knows that you *want* to know whether she's not only enjoying the race but also crossing the finish line.

Realize also that if you two aren't clicking in this area, it's possible other things could be going on. I'm not an expert, and I don't even play one on TV, but if your wife seems to love you but avoids sex (or finds it emotionally painful), make sure there aren't deep-seated issues that need addressing. And if there are, be her advocate in getting the help she needs to address them.

And I know us guys pretend it's never an issue, but if by chance *you're* the one experiencing "performance" problems, be brave and seek help from your doctor or counselor. One woman wrote about this, "His unwillingness to seek medical help is breaking my heart."

You have a lot of life ahead, and your wife wants to enjoy it with you. One wife put it well:

> I appreciate feeling like we are team players not just
> in the bedroom, but in everything. After a long day,

I want to feel supported and uplifted, just as he does. And of course, theoretically, a good roll in the hay will do that! But there are times at the end of the day when I feel as if I can't quite get started. I want him to be sensitive to me and minister to me! He is who I am counting on for this. And I know if I can, he'll be able to count on me, too.

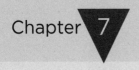

Chapter 7

THE GIRL IN THE MIRROR

What the little girl inside your woman is dying to hear from you—and how to guard your answer well

> *Inside your smart, secure wife lives a little girl who deeply needs to know that you find her beautiful— and that you only have eyes for her.*

As I write this, our daughter is five years old and definitely at that "Daddy's girl" stage. She can whack a pretty good line drive for her age. But she's happiest, I think, when she's dancing for me in the consignment-store costume dress Shaunti bought for her last year. It's pink, and has a twirly skirt.

Pink and twirly matters a lot when you're five. You should see her twirling around our living room. She absolutely beams with delight. Twirl left, pause. Twirl right.

Beauty

149

"Daddy, watch!" she calls as she spins and the skirt does its thing. "Daddy, look at me! Do you think I'm pretty?"

If you've ever had a little girl twirling around your house, you know what I'm thinking right then. *Lord, just let me hold on to this moment! Please...don't let my little girl grow up.*

That's what this chapter is about. Because you see, in a way, little girls never really do.

The Girl Inside

Would it surprise you to know that your gifted, hardworking, secure, grown-up wife is still (silently) asking the same question: "Do you think I'm pretty?" Only now it's you watching. It's you she's asking, and you who will decide her haunting question. Not just "Am I beautiful?" But "*Am I beautiful...to him?*"

In a culture where women are bombarded with expectations to lose weight, look younger, look sexy—actually, look perfect—that question has killer consequences. But it also gives clued-in men an opportunity that we didn't even know we had to affirm our wives in a very important way.

"Am I beautiful...to him?"

On our survey most women told us they had a "deep need or desire" to know that their husband or boyfriend found them beautiful. And younger women were even more likely to have that need. Among women age forty-five and younger, more than three out of four felt this need (77 percent); among women thirty-five and younger the percentage rose to 84 percent.

Regardless of how you think you look, do you have a deep need or desire to know that your husband/significant other finds you beautiful? Which answer most closely describes you? [Choose One Answer]

Women forty-five and younger:

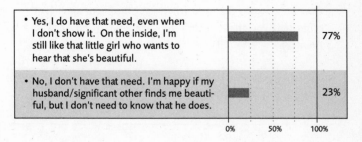

- Yes, I do have that need, even when I don't show it. On the inside, I'm still like that little girl who wants to hear that she's beautiful. — 77%
- No, I don't have that need. I'm happy if my husband/significant other finds me beautiful, but I don't need to know that he does. — 23%

0%   50%   100%

All women:

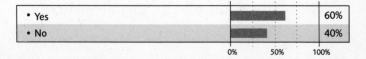

- Yes — 60%
- No — 40%

0%   50%   100%

Beauty

Women with children at home were also much more likely to have a deep desire to hear that their husband found them beautiful—up to 85 percent of them, depending on the age of the kids. One survey taker said the thing she most wished her husband understood was that "women need to be reassured often that they are beautiful and they are loved."

The good news is that when their men *do* tell them they're beautiful, the consequences are…beautiful! Almost 90 percent said it made them feel good or made their day. And that percentage was still huge (77 percent) even among the mostly older women *who said they didn't "need" to hear it!* Only a tiny number (three percent) said it made no difference.

How beneficial is it to you when your husband/significant other tells you that he finds you beautiful? [Choose One Answer]

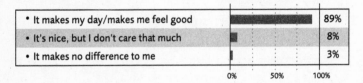

• It makes my day/makes me feel good	89%
• It's nice, but I don't care that much	8%
• It makes no difference to me	3%

One Guy, One Mirror, One Hammer

You might be thinking what Shaunti has already heard from a few skeptical women: Why is this chapter focusing so much on a woman's "looks"? Shouldn't we as a society be getting past that? Well, here's the thing: This *isn't* really about a woman's looks. It *is* about what a woman feels about herself, and the fact that her man has a great ability to build her up in that area or to tear her down.

"Wait a minute!" I can hear you saying. "But she *knows* I think she's beautiful." Well…does she? Have you told her recently? More recently than that time last year when you two got all dressed up for that wedding?

You *did* tell her she looked beautiful then, didn't you? Sure you did.

Okay, you *probably* did.

I, too, think my wife is beautiful, but until Shaunti and I talked about this chapter, I realized that I rarely tell her so. It just wasn't something I thought she needed to hear, or that I needed to do.

Then we talked. Oh boy. All has *not* been well in the land of the free and the home of the Braves.

What I've since learned, and what kept surprising me on our surveys, is that even if a woman knows in her head that her husband finds her beautiful, *she still needs to hear it.* And often. Every day is good.

She still needs to hear it:

- no matter how successful, self-assured or mature she is,

Beauty

- no matter how long you've been together,
- no matter how gorgeous other people might tell her she is,
- no matter how moved to tears of gratitude you were last time you said it,
- no matter how old or young she is...

> "Even if a woman knows in her head that her husband finds her beautiful, *she still needs to hear it.*"

As it turns out, your wife's continuing desire to be beautiful *for you* is a deeply rooted need that explains a lot of other behaviors that have baffled men for centuries.

For example, have you ever wondered:

- Why, after trying on outfit after outfit, she gets frustrated and declares that she "has nothing to wear"?
- Why she wants to buy new clothes even if she knows you all are on a tight budget, or even if few of her clothes could possibly be considered old?
- Why she's always asking you how she looks— when there's a mirror in the bedroom and the bathroom?

- Why she asks, "Do these pants make me look fat?" when what she really means is, "Tell me I'm not fat"?
- Why it's such a big deal if your eyes linger on another beautiful woman?

Listen, after an inexcusably long learning curve, I've come to realize a few crucial facts about beauty and my wife. These facts are fundamental in every marriage, and have the power to radically change your relationship and mine for the better, beginning with the next words you speak to her.

Fact #1. Inside my dear wife, that little dancing girl is still very much alive. Only now she twirls for me.

Fact #2. In our marriage, whether I find her beautiful may or may not be foremost in my mind, but it is an everyday (even if subconscious) issue for her.

Fact #3. In our house, there's really only one mirror. And that mirror is me.

Fact #4. Every day, I can reflect back to her the words she so needs to hear. But if I don't, I leave her vulnerable to both her inner questions and external pressure from an intimidating world.

Beauty

Fact #5. In my hand, I hold a hammer.

I hope you're beginning to see why a clued-in husband or boyfriend can create so much good, and a clueless one can cause so much damage.

And I haven't even told you what the hammer is yet.

> Every day, I can reflect back to her the words she so needs to hear.

The Ugly Truth About Female Beauty in Our World

Just so you and I know that our wives or girlfriends aren't the only "body obsessed" or "oversensitive" women around, let's hear what some women told us about the pressure they feel from our culture and from themselves. It's almost like they must fight their way through a war zone every day—and men don't even realize it. Listen in:

- I know in my head that I am not unattractive. I wouldn't wear a bikini anymore, but people still tell me I'm pretty or that I look really slim in that outfit or whatever. But in my heart, I don't believe it. Because my head is also very aware of all my flaws, especially since the kids came along. Almost every time I see a picture of myself, I cringe inside. I'm guessing that my husband thinks I'm attractive, but I can't think of the last time he made it a point to tell me so. If he would, it sure would counter that secret negativity about myself that I feel inside.

- Every day, we are bombarded with these images all around us of how we are supposed to look. We have this fear that we feel like we'll always have to live up to our husband's expectation of this perfect Hollywood body image and we know we can't do that. And somehow we get this idea that if we don't, oh no, maybe his attention will turn elsewhere. It's a very insecure feeling, even if it's totally ridiculous. We may know in our heads that that's not true, but that "head knowledge" doesn't do anything to counter that silent insecurity.

Beauty

And lastly, here's one that may be hard for any father or married man to hear:

- In this culture, women are not being protected emotionally. They are being humiliated.

Do you really think it is possible for you and me to understand just how "on stage and under review" our wife or girlfriend feels every day? I have to admit—until now I haven't given much thought to how demeaning and threatening our world is for Shaunti and other women. Or really, how demeaning their own internal thoughts about themselves can be, even if they hide it well.

When I think back on typical male responses to this unseen struggle, I'm not encouraged. For Shaunti, I'm the one man in her life who can really relieve the pressure and make her feel beautiful. But because I haven't known I've needed to, my response on an average day to her unseen need has tended to be...a yawn. Or even irritation at how long she's taking to get dressed.

Or on a good day, maybe, "You look nice."

> I'm the one man in her life who can really relieve the pressure and make her feel beautiful.

Guys, we are divinely positioned to encourage and build up the woman we love; we can't be nodding off in the living room chair while the little girl twirls.

So now that we're awake to the problem, what can we do?

Reflecting Back the Truth About Her

Remember, you're not just the guy who shares her space. You're her most important mirror—the man who can reflect back to her how lovely you think she is. The man whose opinions of her are the best antidote for the damaging internal dialogue and external pressure that stalk her thoughts. So how should and could you respond for the greatest benefit to her—and you?

> You're not just the guy who shares her space. You're her most important mirror.

Say it.

Just think of a few affirming words—"You look beautiful today" (or your version thereof)—and *say* them. That kind of compliment might not feel natural to you at first, but if you stick with it, it can eventually feel as familiar as, "Pass the remote."

Whenever possible, your guy-mirror talk should be in specifics. "A lot of women are so desperate for specific, honest compliments," one wife told us. "We're dying of thirst for them. I think guys probably often think them, but don't say them. But I hope they can learn to say them, because one compliment can carry me for a long way."

Beauty

A key time to practice affirmation is when you've both noticed another attractive person. One woman told us: "To me, the confirmation I need is something like this, 'Yes, that other woman is cute, but you're beautiful, and *you're mine*.' Those words would be such a help to me in consciously tearing down the insecurity I carry around."

Say it sincerely.

Words are sweet, but it's your heart she's after. It may sound contradictory to ask you to come up with a "sincere" comment that you wouldn't otherwise have said, but it's just a matter of learning to say what you're already sincerely thinking—just like you would naturally do for your daughter.

> ▽It's just a matter of learning to say what you're already sincerely thinking.

Here's what one woman told us:

I wish I could explain to him that when I'm not satisfied with the options in my closet, what I'm really not satisfied with is myself. I'm bummed that I'm a little overweight, or that my chest is too small, or whatever. At those times, that should be my husband's cue to give me his comments, yes, but not in a clinical way. What I am craving is a sincere, delighted remark from my husband that that red dress looks great on me, shows off my legs, and he's going to have his eyes on me all night!

Say it now.

Most of all, train yourself to say it when she needs it: right away. What she's looking for is the immediate, "reflexive" response that proves you've been wowed. But as this story from one couple we talked to shows, we men have to practice putting ourselves in that frame of mind, lest we send the wrong message!

> Train yourself to say it when she needs it: right away.

Her: After I get ready to go out somewhere, there's sort of a thirty-second rule. If he hasn't noticed me in thirty seconds, I guess I don't look good enough for him. So, okay, we were going out last night. I take a lot of time getting ready and spiffy for him, and I think I look pretty hot. I come downstairs and he doesn't say anything. So instantly, I'm a bit deflated. We walk out of the house and climb into the car,

Beauty

and as we're backing out of the driveway he notices that the little metal insignia on the car hood is crooked. He stops the car and gets out to straighten it. He noticed *that*, but he didn't notice *me*?

Him (laughing ruefully): Pray for me, Jeff!

Erase "fine" from your response options.

Fine is not fine (unless used in the sense, "She's so fine!"). *Fine* is what you mumbled to Mom when she asked you how school went.

One wife mentioned that if she asked at the beginning of an evening out how she looked, her husband would typically say, "You look fine, sweetheart." But as she put it, "I worked this hard for *fine*?"

I think guys say that word because we simply misunderstand the real question. When she asks how she looks, we think she's wondering if she looks presentable. But what she wants to know is if she's still rocking our world—like she did on that first date. So "fine," sort of by definition, tells her, "No, you're not rocking my world."

> What she wants to know is if she's still rocking our world.

Don't take "no" for an answer.

By now, you might be thinking, *But I try to compliment my wife—and she always brushes it off!* At those times, you probably give up, thinking she doesn't need affirmation or that there's no point in expending the energy if she's not going to believe it.

Pointer from Shaunti: Take her reluctance as a sign that she needs the affirmation even more. It may not look like it, but she's probably reacting out of discomfort with compliments, or even a painful personal awareness of her flaws. Remember, her flaws loom very large in her mind. Even if you hardly notice them, it's hard for her to believe that. So keep telling her, and she'll learn to relax and believe that you mean it.

What if I *do* agree there's an area to work on?

Most men have probably known the deer-in-the-headlights feeling when a woman is dissatisfied with her weight and wants to talk about it—and you really don't. There really *is* no way to talk about it without hurting her feelings, unless she's specifically asked you and given you permission to be honest for some compelling reason. (Like, "Promise me that you'll tell me if I shouldn't wear that dress, so I don't embarrass myself at the reunion.")

Beauty

If she's struggling with something that is a real issue (like she's twenty-five pounds overweight) instead of just being dissatisfied with something she can't healthfully change (she thinks her nose is too big), realize that she feels terrible about it already. Knowing you are disappointed, too, makes it worse. That said, if she makes comments about wanting to lose weight—and you think she's seriously contemplating making a change and inviting your thoughts—be supportive and *ask how you can help*. Good sentence starters: "I love you no matter what. But if this bothers you...how can I help?" Then, be willing to help—whether that means doing the soccer run so she can hit the gym or forgoing your nightly ice cream if it tempts her too much. Encourage the results of her efforts! And always affirm those areas that you *do* find beautiful, including her loveliness as a person.

> Always affirm those areas that you *do* find beautiful, including her loveliness as a person.

Also, remember that for her, knowing that you find her lovely not just on the outside, but the inside as well, will go a long way. We've all seen examples where an otherwise plain looking woman became absolutely beautiful in our eyes because she had the "beauty of a quiet and gentle spirit," as the apostle Peter put it. If your wife is a lovely person but knows that her teeth are crooked or her post-childbearing stomach is no longer flat, tell her—often—that you truly don't notice what she thinks of as flaws. Tell her that her inner loveliness radiates through her, and that you—and everyone else—find her beautiful.

View cost as an investment.

A lot of husbands struggle with their wives' desire to spend money on clothes, makeup, or beauty treatments. I hope by now you're seeing what's really happening here—she's trying to stay in the center of your field of vision and to bolster her own internal gauge of how she feels about herself.

No one is saying households should throw budget caution out the window. But what might appear a "nonessential" to us men might be a budget priority for her that she is willing to make trade-offs for. Here's a note Shaunti received on this topic:

> Please explain to the guys how important clothes are to women. Please try to explain how frumpy and unattractive we feel in old clothes, whether they are

Beauty

worn out or just out of date. A couple of my best friends struggle with this in their marriages; it's a common problem.

Interestingly, according to Shaunti's research for *For Women Only*, most men are very willing to spend time or money to support a wife's weight loss or fitness program—for example, by watching the kids or paying for a gym membership. We *do* make the beauty connection at one level, where it matters to us. We just need to make that connection where it matters to *her*.

Now it's time to squarely address what may be the most important beauty connection of all. Because you and I can do an excellent job of reflecting our wife's beauty back to her and *still* cause enormous damage.

How?

Fact #5: In my hand, I hold a hammer.

The Hammer Drops: Looking Elsewhere

We now know that women are powerfully affirmed by knowing that their husband finds them beautiful. But that power has a dark side. Because if a woman sees her husband's eyes *also* affirming the beauty of other women, she ceases to feel special. And suddenly, not only is she not affirmed, she's in competition with the world again—including for the attentions of the one man she thought she already had. That's when the hammer hits the mirror of you—the most important mirror in her life—and shatters it.

> If a woman sees her husband's eyes also affirming the beauty of other women, she ceases to feel special.

Now, because women are not as visually wired as we are, there are bound to be some misunderstandings here—some conflicts between what we consider "innocent" and what our women think. We may think, "My wife knows it's just a guy thing and that I don't love this other woman I'm looking at." We've even coined some analogies that elevate staring to a noble level: "It's like enjoying a beautiful painting in a museum," we say. "Just don't try and take the picture home."

Yes, sometimes it can simply be admiring beauty. And yes, God has created a beautiful world—and populating it with attractive people is consistent with His artistry. But the challenge with looking at a beautiful woman is the speed at which admiration morphs into something else. Looking at the sweeping vista of the Rockies just doesn't run the risk of

Beauty

my next thought being, "I wonder what those mountains would look like without all that snow on them."

I'm not going to spend the rest of this chapter talking about how we need to keep our thought lives pure, since I think most of us already know that, whether consciously or subconsciously. (Still, I strongly urge you: Don't settle for what you have considered unavoidable or even normal on this temptation. "Do not conform any longer to the pattern of this world, but be transformed by the renewing of your mind" (Romans 12:2). I believe that through God's power, not our own, we *can* be transformed. And if you need outside resources, there are many great ones today, including *Every Man's Battle* by Stephen Arterburn and Fred Stoeker and *Sex Is Not the Problem (Lust Is)* by Joshua Harris.) My main purpose is to help motivated, sensitive, and slightly clueless guys like you and me become more motivated, more sensitive, and slightly less clueless husbands by explaining what is going on *inside our wives*.

The hard truth is, most women *don't* just dismiss our sideways glances as "a guy thing." Look at what one woman wrote us:

I haven't been able to come to grips with my husband looking at other women. He is not into pornography, for which I am so thankful, but sometimes I see him looking for quite a bit longer than just a glance at other, younger women. I cannot describe the hurt I feel when he allows his eyes to take in every detail. I think otherwise very wonderful men don't stop to think about how this makes a woman feel. That figure my husband is looking at clarifies for me his deepest physical desires—and I look nothing like that. This leaves me feeling like I can never be what my loved one *really* wants.

It's news to them...

I was also surprised at how many women had no idea that our visual wiring makes it difficult to *not* notice other women— and how many women have a really hard time with that knowledge. As one wife said:

> I find it more than slightly threatening to know that no matter how much I work to be the woman of his dreams, my husband will always feel the pull from others. I appreciate the fact that he struggles to keep his mind on me, but just the fact that he has to struggle at all is so hard for me. It is very difficult to accept the fact that while I can be totally possessed, I can never completely possess.

Beauty

Remember, women *already* feel that they are in competition with every other beautiful woman—real or imagined—out there. Many women have told Shaunti and me that it's not that they walk around feeling violently suspicious of where we are looking as much as that they know they live in a culture saturated with options other than *them*. Shapelier options, racier options, younger options, easier options—and they're now aware that *the man they love is wired to notice every option*. So when he does, it's hurtful.

> Women already feel that they are in competition with every other beautiful woman—real or imagined—out there.

When the mirror shatters

On our survey for this book, although two-thirds of women said they'd be bothered if their man noticed a woman with a great body, only one out of four said they'd be hurt. But when we asked how they'd feel *if they knew their man's thoughts were lingering on that woman's body*, the number of women who said they'd be hurt jumped to three out of four, with even higher rates among women under age forty-five. (Shaunti suspects that these numbers would be even higher if women could actually see inside our heads and watch our thoughts like a movie, and I do, too.)

Imagine you are sitting with your husband/significant other in a train station and a woman with a great body walks in and stands in a nearby line. Your husband/significant other glances at her several times and appears quite distracted by her. How does this make you feel? [Choose One Answer]*

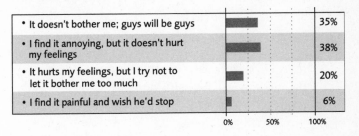

• It doesn't bother me; guys will be guys	35%
• I find it annoying, but it doesn't hurt my feelings	38%
• It hurts my feelings, but I try not to let it bother me too much	20%
• I find it painful and wish he'd stop	6%

0%   50%   100%

Now imagine that in that same situation, you could magically see inside your husband/significant other's head. If you were to find out that his thoughts were lingering on that woman's body, would you find it hurtful? [Choose One Answer]

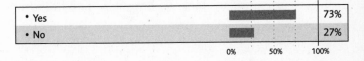

• Yes	73%
• No	27%

0%   50%   100%

* Because of rounding, numbers don't quite reach 100%.

Truth is, most women can't comprehend why a man would choose or risk such damage. For many, lingering thoughts

Beauty

(and, lets just admit it, lusting) were the same thing as cheating. "A woman whose husband doesn't control his looking and lusting will start to feel like a failure," one wife told us. "Why shouldn't she? Her beauty can no longer measure up to what her husband wants. His eyes speak volumes, so she has no choice but to doubt. But *she* wants to be found worthy in his eyes, *she* wants to be his beauty."

> "A woman whose husband doesn't control his looking will feel she doesn't measure up to what he wants."

As a man who, like you, wants to honor and show love to his wife, I find that woman's comment—and literally hundreds more like it—very sobering. While most women don't mind if a husband or boyfriend is truly appreciating beauty (as in, "What a beautiful girl!"), they experience excruciating pain if we look at, linger on, and lust after another attractive female. Their trust in their man's love gets badly shaken.

Shaking turns to breaking when the other woman or image obviously aims to *provoke* lust. That brings us to porn.

"Porn sends her a clear message..."

"Let's face it," wrote one woman, "my husband can't control what woman will show up at what store or what street at a given time. It's not as though he's wishing that woman to appear. Porn, however, is different. Porn is a conscious choice. I think that when a man turns to porn, no matter how infrequently, it sends a clear message to his wife that she is inadequate. It says that no matter how she tries, she can't satisfy him sexually. Why should she bother trying?"

Unless a woman is naive about the power of porn or has become desensitized to it for other reasons, when her husband uses porn, it *feels* like cheating. And in truth, it *is* cheating. (Jesus' words come to mind here: "Anyone who looks at a woman lustfully has already committed adultery with her in his heart.") Even wives who don't equate using pornography with adultery find the experience excruciating.

The fact is, for all men, this is an area where there really has to be zero tolerance. Obviously that applies to pornography. But it also applies to lingering glances and lustful thoughts. We injure our wife when we look elsewhere for a thrill that we vowed to look for only in her. We shatter our ability to reflect her beauty back to her. And we break her trust.

Beauty

We Can Send Her Another Message

Since our wife needs to know that we find her beautiful, and she feels protected by knowing that we only have eyes for her, well…we have plenty of opportunities these days to send her that message.

In the mid-'90s, *Sports Illustrated* did a cover feature, entitled, "St. David," on David Robinson, the MVP center for the San Antonio Spurs. One segment described how Robinson handled himself, as a professing Christian, husband, and father, in the midst of the NBA's intense temptations. For example, during television breaks, he would sit on the bench and stare studiously at the floor in order to avoid looking at the gyrating cheerleaders out on the court.

The article also mentioned that like all NBA players, Robinson was constantly approached by attractive women who wanted to talk to him…and were probably offering more than just witty conversation. Apparently, he would rather brusquely brush them off. When asked to comment on that seemingly "rude" practice, he said something like this: "If any woman is going to get her feelings hurt, *it's not going to be my wife.*"

A protector and hero in action.

> "If any woman is going to get her feelings hurt, *it's not going to be my wife.*"

Each day your wife and mine hold out to us their intense, God-given, little-girl desire (and right) to be treasured. Each day she's threatened on all sides by an offensive and abusive world. And each day—with kind words and faithful eyes—we, too, can be our wife's protector and hero.

Beauty

Chapter 8

THE MAN SHE HAD HOPED TO MARRY

What the woman who loves you most, most wants you to know

In just a moment, I'll share my biggest surprise from all my "embedded male" research in interviews, surveys, and websites. But before I do, I want to take you to a different data bank entirely—the mailbag from wives and girlfriends who wrote and e-mailed Shaunti after reading *For Women Only*. Overwhelmingly, they relayed two things: how much they didn't know that they didn't know, and how much the relationship had changed once they understood their man's inner life—and started doing things differently.

The Change in Two
That Starts with One

At various points in this book, you may have found yourself saying, "But if she would only be *reasonable*, I wouldn't have to do all this stuff you're telling me!" We sympathize with that sentiment because Shaunti and I have each felt it at one time or another in our *own* learning process!

So many of the women who wrote in to Shaunti described the same feeling—"This is unfair, why do I have to do all the work?"—as well as how they came out the other side. Look at this excerpt from one e-mail:

> I fought my urge to defend myself and prayed that God would open my heart to consider the possibility that it was me, not my husband, who needed to change. And of course I immediately realized that was true. I was frustrated to know that I had behaved this way for five years of our marriage. But by the end of the book, I "owned" it. And I also realized that if I had the power to destroy my marriage, I now have the power to change and build it up again!

Guys, we could say the same thing. We don't have to wait until she completely understands us to see positive results. Now that we have more clarity about several key areas of her inner life and needs, the ball is in our court. We've now seen over and over that you can be the only person to change in your relationship and *still* expect great new beginnings. Your marriage is definitely worth you taking the first step.

⚠ The ball is in our court.

Which leads me to the biggest surprise of all.

The one most important thing...

As you can imagine, being the "embedded male" gave me lots of opportunities to be surprised. But nothing can compare to how I felt when I looked at the end of the survey. After two dozen multiple-choice questions, we gave the survey takers a blank space and asked: "What's the most important thing you wish your husband/significant other knew, but feel you haven't been able to explain in a way he understands?"

I assumed that the women would have plenty to say about what their husband didn't understand, and in all honesty I had to gather my courage to look at the responses. And then I was astonished. Because the top thing that women wished their man knew was this:

You are my hero.

Conclusion

Not always in those exact words, mind you, but invariably with that exact meaning. Over and over again, when women could say anything, they tried to express just how central their man was in their life, how much they admired, appreciated, and needed him, how much they wanted to make him happy, and how grateful they were for such a wonderful husband.

They were saying, in essence, that their husband really *is* the man that they had hoped he would be when they married him. Their average, ordinary guy—the person who sometimes leaves his fly down and the toilet seat up—*is* their knight in shining armor.

Look at what this survey taker said she most wished her husband knew:

That he has made me the happiest woman in the world. I could have never asked for anything more. His love and support throughout our marriage is more than any woman could want. I am so lucky to have found him thirty-two years ago.

"He has made me the happiest woman in the world. I could have never asked for anything more."

There's no way in this short space to give you the same sense of surprise that I had as I sat at my computer and scrolled down so many similar survey responses. Here are just a few examples:

- How deep my love and respect is for him.
- How much I appreciate him.
- How much I care for his happiness, feelings, and well-being.
- How much I respect him as a person.
- I would trust him with my life.
- My husband means more to me than words can say. He is the true essence of what I dreamed a husband would be when I was a little girl.
- That I dearly appreciate his hard work.
- That I feel incredibly lucky to be with him today.
- When he puts himself down it hurts me—no one should say bad things about my favorite guy.

They Feel It but Don't Always Know How to Show It

I had been skeptical when Shaunti proposed this idea, but she suspected from her talks at women's groups around the country that *most* women really do feel great respect and appreciation for their husband or boyfriend but don't always *show* it. Often, women simply don't realize that some of their words or actions actually convey a lack of trust, when, as she says, "that is not the way they feel *at all!*"

So on the survey, we decided to ask the question directly and see what happened. Shaunti guessed that at least nine out of ten women would jump at the chance to confirm that they *did* respect and appreciate their husband or boyfriend...and she was right.

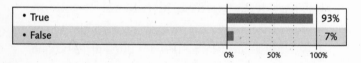

Is this statement true or false? "Although I may not always show it well, I do deeply need, respect, and desire, my husband/significant other." [Choose One Answer]*

• True	93%
• False	7%

0%   50%   100%

*Excludes divorced/separated women (who *still* answered in the 80% range!).

In closing...

I will leave you with this comment from one woman who spoke for many in trying to describe just how important her husband is to her:

> My husband smiles at me when he comes home from work and discovers the kids have drawn monsters on my legs with markers. He appreciates egg sandwiches and SpaghettiOs more than a gourmet meal. He believes that I am a better mother, more talented, and a more virtuous person than I actually am...His eternal optimism changes me ever so slightly, day after day, into something much more beautiful than I'd otherwise be. He's imperfect, puerile, and sloppy, yet strong, wise, and loving.
>
> The fact that I get to live with him over the course of my lifetime is one of the biggest scams I've pulled off—I keep waiting for him to wake up, jump over the mound of unwashed clothes, and bolt out the door. But he sees even my imperfections as endearing. Over the past ten years, we've both changed. But the one thing that remains constant is my utter and unashamed need of him.
>
> Not to mention, he's really good in the sack.

Conclusion

A Final Note...

As Shaunti noted up front, men often process new information differently than women do, mulling things over internally and perhaps investigating perplexing topics more closely. We urge any women sneaking a peek at this book to give their men the space and time that they will need to process, and recognize that they may not actually want to talk about it—they may simply want to practice it!

For men who want to learn about certain areas in more detail, we list additional resources at www.formenonlybook.com. One good "next step" is Emerson Eggerichs's book *Love and Respect*, particularly the chapters written for men.

CITATIONS

Chapter 2

Source for footnote: Emerson Eggerichs, *Love and Respect* (Brentwood, TN: Integrity Publishers, 2004).

Movie dialogue is from *The Parent Trap*, directed by Nancy Meyers (Disney, 1998); cast, Dennis Quaid and Natasha Richardson.

Chapter 6

Information demonstrating that husbands who do more chores tend to have more and better sex comes from John Gottman, PhD, and Nan Silver, *The Seven Principles for Making Marriage Work* (New York: Random House), 205–206.

Source for footnote 2: Dr. Douglas Rosenau, *A Celebration of Sex* (Nashville: Thomas Nelson, 2002), 168, 214–215.

Source for footnote 3: Theresa Crenshaw, *Alchemy of Love and Lust* (New York: Simon & Schuster, 1996), 125.

Chapter 7

David Robinson quote from Leigh Montville, "The Trials of David," Sports Illustrated, April 29, 1996, 95. Full quote: "I made a rule when I got married.... I decided that if anyone's feelings are going to be hurt, they're not going to be my wife's. If I think [a woman] is acting inappropriately, I say so. It may sound harsh, but that's the way it is. My wife is not going to be the one to suffer."

ACKNOWLEDGMENTS

Literally thousands of people provided the input and assistance that was crucial to the writing and content of this book, and there is no way to adequately thank them in this short space. To all of these wonderful folks, we want to say thank you, and ask forgiveness in advance if we leave anyone out of this section.

First we must deeply thank and acknowledge our prayer team, who did the real work of this book by covering us in prayer for most of a year: Martha and Barry Abrams, Kurt Alme, Diana Baker, Elizabeth Beinhocker, Michael and Deon Brown, Ann Browne, Mark and Christa Crawford, Gerry and Kasey Crete, Alison Darrell, Mike Deagle, Betty Dunkum, Calvin Edwards, Craig and Lynn Elam, Mollianne Elliott, Darby Ferguson, Susan Fleck, Larissa Fontenot, Nancy French, Lisa and Ron Fry, Natt and Meredith Gantt, Kate Gates, Dan Glaze, Michael and Debra Goldstone, Jennifer Graves, Laura Grindley, Dean and Jan Harbry, Judy Hitson, John and Monica Holcomb, Lin Hopkins, Anne Hotchkiss, Victor Jih, Jane Joiner, Audrey Lambert, Kristen Lambert,

Mary Laudermilk, Charl and Elsa Liebenberg, Jan and John MacLaury, Karen McAdams, Kurt Montavon, Lisa and John Nagle, Bruce and Sue Osterink, Darlene Penner, Elizabeth Noller, Linda and Jack Preston, Dick and Judy Reidinger, Eric and Lisa Rice, Phil and Susan Rodenberg, Andy and Jeanne Sandecki, Roger Scarlett, Albert and Wendy Shashoua, Jim and Chris Sharp, Jenny Shea, D. J. Snell, Lon and Katherine Waitman, and Ed and Jewels Warren.

The professional survey of women that is at the core of this book was guided by the experienced hand of Chuck Cowan of Analytic Focus (analyticfocus.com), and performed by Kevin Sharp and the rest of the team at Decision Analyst (decisionanalyst.com). As in previous books, I thank this excellent team.

We promised to keep the identity of the interviewees and focus group participants confidential, so we cannot name them here. But please know just how much we appreciate all of you. We also are so appreciative of the many women's group directors and conference organizers that have invited Shaunti to speak, allowing her to test and refine our emerging findings in the process.

Several individuals went above and beyond in providing assistance and help as we investigated the topics covered in this book. We need to especially acknowledge counselors Chris and Susan Silver of Tree of Life Ministries and Atlanta-based sex therapists and experts Dr. Douglas Rosenau and Dr. Michael Sytsma.

We are very grateful for the team that has come alongside to support and encourage us personally and professionally, especially Shaunti's assistants Jeanne Sandecki and Maylynn Wilson, and her project manager, Linda Crews. We are also indebted to our special friends Eric and Lisa Rice, whose input, encouragement, and friendship was invaluable during this process. Thanks also to Dan Knutson and his excellent staff at Higher Grounds in Duluth, GA, who allowed Shaunti to camp out at their coffee shop for months at a time while writing.

We are not quite sure how to adequately thank our exceptional editors, Dave and Heather Kopp, who went way, *way* above and beyond the call of duty, particularly the unexpected duty of taking a huge manuscript and turning it into a book that someone might actually be willing to read. To both of you: We are so grateful for your professional skills, your encouragement, and your friendship. We are also immensely grateful to Don Jacobson and rest of the Multnomah family for their incredible friendship, support, and excellence. You all are such a pleasure to work with!

We also must express our incredible gratitude to our parents, to whom this book is dedicated: Bill and Roberta Feldhahn, and Richard and Judy Reidinger. You know we could never have written this book without each of you, who rode to the rescue time and again to help with kids, household chores, and editing input while deadlines loomed. We love each of you very much and are immensely grateful for your presence in our lives.

To our children: Thank you for being such good little peanuts, and understanding when Mom or Dad had to be locked away with a computer for hours at a time. We adore you, and are so proud of the young lady and young man you are becoming.

Finally, and most importantly, we lift up all praise and honor to the One who truly deserves it. If there is any eye-opening power in this book, it is because of the anointing of the Lord, who cares for His children and wants their relationships to be filled with joy.

"If you've ever asked, 'Why does she do, think, or say that?' then you've got to read this book. Shaunti and Jeff not only answer this question, they eliminate the confusion that has kept far too many men from bridging the gender gap."

—DRS. LES AND LESLIE PARROTT
Bestselling authors of *Love Talk*

"When we featured Shaunti's book *For Women Only* on *FamilyLife Today*, the phone rang off the hook! When Shaunti and Jeff come back on our broadcast, I'm buying some more phones. This is fresh and relevant—good stuff for every marriage. Read it!"

—DENNIS RAINEY
President, FamilyLife

"Once again Shaunti and Jeff Feldhahn have unearthed a treasure chest of insights that are not only eye-opening, but possibly life-changing."

—ANDY STANLEY
North Point Ministries senior pastor and bestselling author

"Most of my work helping passive Christian men become more like Jesus involves how best to relate to women. I'm going to make sure to keep a case of the Feldhahn's excellent book handy at all times."

—PAUL COUGHLIN
Author, *No More Christian Nice Guy* and *Married But Not Engaged*